CW01083278

Wine Not?
A Whimsical Journey Through the World of Wine

A Humorous Deep-Dive into the Intricacies of the World's Favorite Elixir

---

By

Dr. U

Table of Contents

Foreword

Oh, the illustrious world of wine! A realm where grapes metamorphose into liquid eloquence, and every bottle narrates a tale of soils kissed by sun and rain. However, as our humble grape journeys from vine to vintage, it often gets enrobed in a lexicon so grand, it would make a dictionary blush! The simple joy of sipping wine metamorphoses into a grandiloquent gala of 'tannins', 'terroirs', and 'bouquets'. But worry not, for Dr. U. is here to rescue us from the vineyards of verbosity and lead us into meadows of mirth.

As you open this book, you're not just uncorking a collection of pages, but a new perspective that marries merriment to Merlot, hilarity to Chardonnay, and giggles to Cabernet. Dr. U. embarks on a whimsical expedition to demystify the often intimidating jargon of the wine world and replaces it with laughter, tales of amusing misadventures, and a lexicon that's as refreshing as a chilled glass of Riesling on a warm summer day.

This is not a book that aims to transform you into a sommelier overnight (though a miracle might just do the trick!). Rather, it's your companion in turning wine tasting from a 'highbrow hobby' to a 'heartfelt hilarity'. Through the pages, you'll navigate supermarket aisles with a grin, explore vineyards with a chuckle, and even wrestle with wine labels, all the while laughing at the amusing anecdotes and whimsical wisdom that Dr. U. shares from his own journey of exploring the wine world one sip, one chuckle at a time.

Dr. U.'s narrative is a delightful detour from the beaten path of wine elitism, leading you into a realm where wine is not a whisper among the elite, but a conversation starter for all. It's about embracing the joy of discovery, the fun of learning, and of course, the universal language of laughter that binds us all.

So, dear reader, as you flip through these pages, prepare to swirl, sniff, and sip through the whimsical world of wine, but with a dash of humor, a pinch of playfulness, and a generous pour of joviality. The expedition from grape to glass has never been more gigglesome. Uncork the book, pour yourself a glass, and let the vinous voyage of vivacity begin!

About the author

At 'daytime' Dr. U. has an interesting and demanding profession which he really loves, but 'after hours', this very curious Dr. U. always aims to expand his horizon. Aims to disover new territories, new horizons and always trying something new. And he found a new passion. Wine.

Dr. U. is not your everyday connoisseur of wine; rather, a passionate aficionado on a quest for vinous wisdom, with a heart full of laughter and a glass forever half-full. His journey into the realm of wine began not in a sophisticated wine tasting course, but amidst the aisles of everyday supermarkets, with a curiosity as fine as a vintage Merlot.

The world of wine, often veiled in a shroud of elite jargon and pretentious aura, tickled both his humor and his quest for knowledge. Dr. U. found the irony in the narrative that veiled the simplicity and essence of wine behind a facade of complex terminology accessible only to the so-called connoisseurs. With every sip, he peeled away layers of pretension, finding a narrative that was as real as it was refreshing.

This book is not just a whimsical expedition from grape to glass; it's a narrative that seeks to uncork the elitism bottled up in the world of wine. With a humorous quill, Dr. U. decants the essence of wine, making it an accessible, enjoyable, and educative experience for all. His tales are not of an expert, but of a lover of life, laughter, and the lingering taste of a good wine.

The author believes that the beauty of wine lies in its ability to bring people together, to spark conversations, and to enrich our lives with flavors and stories. His narrative is a toast to every individual who has felt lost in the sophisticated jargon of the wine world. He invites you to a journey where every page is a step towards demystifying the vinous vernacular, making wine a simple, laughable, and enjoyable aspect of everyday life.

As you traverse through the pages, you will find in Dr. U. a companion who shares your quest for simplicity amidst the complex aroma of wines, a humorist who finds joy in every sip, and a learner who believes that the world of wine is a grand narrative waiting to be shared and enjoyed by all, one laugh at a time.

Navigating the Wine Aisle: A First-Time Adventure

Navigating the supermarket

Let's begin with a playful look at the deceptive nature of wine labels. The sheer range of wine packaging, with its spectrum of bottle shapes, colors and creative designs, can leave an amateur shopper's head spinning. The trick is not to fall for the age-old trap of "ooh, that's a pretty label!" and to beware the wine that hides behind a facade of artistic intrigue or over-the-top stylishness. Instead, visualize yourself as a spy in the world of wine, where you carefully decode the information on the label and stealthily draw conclusions on the delicious contents inside.

As you venture down the wine aisle, be on the lookout for regional renegades masquerading as their more renowned cousins. These wines may tempt shoppers with the lure of well-known locales, only to reveal a geographic twist upon closer inspection. For example, a Californian wine cheekily mimicking a French Bordeaux might leave your taste buds in quite the conundrum. Embrace the exciting challenge of uncovering these surprising finds! Who knows? You might just discover a delightful, lesser-known wine in doing so.

Next up are the quirky titles and baffling slang printed on wine labels, which can render even trivial decision-making into an ambiguous, Herculean task. Terms like "neo-gothic," "rockstar," and "punk princess" might tickle your funny bone but offer little insight into the wine's flavor. Appreciate the humor in these terms, but do not let them sway your decision. Instead, focus on eye-catching phrases embedded in the small print, such as "single-vineyard," "estate-grown," or "old vines," which often indicate a more unique and potentially tastier wine.

At the supermarket, wine pricing can be quite the circus. High price tags instill the fear that we must pay a fortune for a decent wine, while low-cost bottles prod at our inner bargain hunters. Yet, the correlation between price and quality is a fascinating enigma. Embrace the price-shuffle as a hilarious game of wits, and remember that great taste can emerge from both the budget and luxury realms. To increase your chances of finding a winner at any price, keep an eye out for discount promotions on higher-priced wines and hone your detective skills on the "bargain-bin."

When confronted with a never-ending row of wines, sometimes the only defense we have against decision fatigue is a hearty laugh about the absurdity of it all. But what if we let our imaginations run wild and envisioned wine selection as a dating game? Each bottle vies for your attention, trying to charm you with its wit, sophistication, and sultry seductions. Put your match-making skills to the test, and let loose with humorous (wholesome) wine bottle conversations in your mind, remembering that the ultimate decision is yours!

Now that our wine selection adventure is reaching its pinnacle, it's time to propel you forth with some well-earned advice: trust your instincts. Wear your amateur status like a badge of honor, rather than a scarlet letter; after all, you have a fresh, untainted perspective on the world of wine, and your choices will only grow sharper over time as you become well-versed in the subtle intricacies of the wine aisle. Your gut feeling might not have the expertise of an experienced sommelier, but it knows your taste buds better than anyone.

As we conclude our supermarket soiree and approach the till with our precious cargo, remember that humor has been your faithful guide. May the wine you've chosen be not only the result of an entertaining and stress-free shopping trip but also serve as a reminder that the journey is just as important as the destination.

Laugh! You ventured forth into the confusing and overwhelming terrain of wine buying and emerged triumphant, armed with newfound knowledge and an unquenchable thirst for more exploration. Though our journey together may end here, your future escapades in the wine aisle now hold endless possibilities for discovery, humor, and joy. Go forth, intrepid shoppers, and relish in the delights offered by the world of wine! And when in doubt, remember that laughter just might be the most dependable wine pairing of all.

Survival Guide: Comically Navigating the Wine Aisle

Ah, the wine aisle: that wondrous but confounding labyrinth of bottles where intoxicating nectar awaits within a sea of grape-based delights. It is a siren's call for any amateur wine lover, beckoning the hapless consumer toward its bewitching arms while harboring a kaleidoscope of confounding dilemmas that would baffle even the most seasoned adventurers. Fear not, for even in this bewildering terrain, there is a saving grace: humor! Allow me to guide you through this comical but educational journey as we venture through the wine aisle of your local supermarket and emerge unscathed, armed with newfound knowledge and a palate primed for pleasure.

As we begin our expedition, the first thing that strikes us is the plethora of labels and bottles vying for our undivided attention. Bizarrely, they all seem to possess a Dr. Jekyll and Mr. Hyde persona. On one hand, they offer the promise of complex flavors, sophisticated undertones, and tantalizing bouquets; on the other hand, they are riddled with cryptic terminology, vague descriptions, and outlandish claims that challenge the limits of comprehension. Fortunately, our secret weapon—humor—provides us with a laughable lens through which to view these perplexing paradoxes. Armed with curiosity and an arsenal of chuckles, let's tackle the challenge of decoding these vinous enigmas on our daring supermarket escapade.

Approaching the wine aisle, we must first conquer our fear of intimidation. Standing before endless rows of bottles, it's easy to feel like a helpless child lost in the sardonic amusement park of wine. Even Aladdin's magic lamp, with the promise of a genie's three wishes, might not be enough to grant us the clarity to navigate through such a bewildering bazaar. Indeed, many a wise sage would wisely suggest that the key to survival in this treacherous terrain lies within us all. We must trust our instincts, engage our sense of humor, and face the challenge head-on.

To begin our pilgrimage, banish the notion that there is a "right" or "wrong" choice in the wine aisle. This will only serve to stifle your sense of adventure and hinder any inclination toward discovery and learning. Surrender to the idea that the world of wine is subjective, and that finding the perfect bottle is sometimes akin to landing on the proverbial goldilocks scenario. Embrace the idea that your choice need not be governed only by expert advice or rigorous rules, but also by the delightful interplay of personal preference, whimsy, and yes, humor.

One way to approach your wine selection is to view it as a game—one where the objective is to develop your palate, expand your knowledge, and have a laugh, all while vying for temporary bragging rights in your circle of friends. Don't be daunted by the vast sea of bottles; rather, think of them as contestants in a playful episode of "The Bachelor," each vying for your favor and validation. Imagine each label as a dating profile, complete with glamorous photos, witty banter, and occasionally inflated claims of grandiosity.

But remember, with great power comes great responsibility: choosing the right companion for your palate is your task alone. Use your intuition, examine the label's content, and consider the context in which you'll be enjoying your wine. Will it be a cozy night at home binge-watching your favorite series, an intimate dinner with a special someone, or a raucous potluck gathering with friends? By considering the overall experience, you'll narrow your choices and leave the wine aisle positively gleeful.

Our journey through the wine aisle ultimately comes down to one simple thing: trusting your gut. Focus on the pleasure of learning and discovery, and remember that each bottle, whether it delights or disappoints, is an opportunity to grow and expand your personal wine universe. Allow humor to be your trusted ally, imparting the confidence to make informed choices without becoming overwhelmed or paralyzed with indecision.

As we exit the wine aisle, treasure trove of bottles in tow, a triumphant smile creeps upon our faces. The wine spectrum brims with a wealth of unexpected pleasures, nuanced tastes, and diverse histories. The allure of wine lies not only in the pursuit of discovering new flavors but also in the amusement that awaits each of us in our own inimitable wine selections, which charm our taste buds and broaden our personal horizons.

So, let us toast to our unique journey in search of the ultimate elixir, and remember that the swirl of laughter and experimentation on our lips is the true essence of wine.

Hitting the Shelves: A Whimsical Wine Shopping Adventure

Picture this: a vast mountain range of wine bottles sprawling across a labyrinth of supermarket shelves, their labels possessing both the charm of ancient poetry and the confusion of modern art. As we embark upon this whimsical adventure, we may feel as if we've wandered into some surreal landscape where curiosity and courage are our only compass.

Within this enchanting terrain, we encounter a motley assortment of bottle shapes, ranging from elegant to downright odd. Syrah, with its sensuous curves, woos us from its shelf, while a minimalist bottle of Chenin Blanc whispers sweet nothings of sophistication in our ear. Spherical bottles of late harvest Vidal beckon us toward their gaudy kingdom, while the humble Jug of Carlo Rossi offers a comforting hug of familiarity.

As we peruse the almost-endless library of labels, let us cast a light circus of humor on the drama that unfolds. Wine labels may weave tantalizing tales of romance, adventure, and mystery, but what lies beneath the surface may not always be what it seems. An unfamiliar grape varietal bearing a curious name may awaken our inner explorer, while a wine with an iconic brand may try to convince us that we should pay the modern-day equivalent of a king's ransom merely due to the prestige it carries.

Our journey continues with an exploration of the enigmatic language of wine labels. Be it a cryptic assertion of the wine's terroir, a riddle of taste descriptions, or a tongue-in-cheek homage to antiquity, these phrases spark our imaginations and coax our senses. Verbiage such as "twilight berry" or "espresso conspiracy" entices us to voyage further into a realm of aesthetic romanticism, even if the actual palate profile might leave us perplexed.

And what of those vintage years and varietals that command a near-encyclopedic knowledge? The haunting refrain of a 1961 Bordeaux echoes amongst the dusty shelves, while a 2010 Brunello di Montalcino lies dormant like a forgotten Italian villa. And then there are varietals that perplex and delight with their exotic names such as Tannat, Assyrtiko, and Xinomavro - a linguistic menagerie of titillating possibilities.

Standing before this cavalcade of vinous wonderment, we may feel overwhelmed and vulnerable. We must remember, however, that every journey of a thousand wines begins with a single sip. Courage lies within our hearts as we embrace the delightful unpredictability of our wine shopping escapades. With warmth, wit, and a dose of curiosity, we embark upon this odyssey with the fragrant memories of past encounters and the bittersweet anticipation of future delights.

As we traverse this delightful yet puzzling terrain, we find a curious truth: the essence of wine is not to be found merely in the swirl of its flavors or the weight of its color, but also within the alchemy of human connection and shared laughter. For in the end, whether we select a bottle of Prosecco that pirouettes on the rim of a champagne flute or a robust Malbec that warms our souls, the greatest story that wine has to tell lies in the shared experiences and humor that we enjoy with our friends and family.

So, my fellow adventurers, fret not if the words and pictures on the wine labels befuddle you or the sheer array of choices besets you with indecision. For in this whimsical wine shopping adventure, it is ultimately the laughter and camaraderie that we share along the journey that will make each glass a delightful, memorable, and, dare I say, intoxicating experience.

As we leave the wine aisle, hearts full of amusement and anticipation, may we remember the spirit of our whimsical adventure as we cheers to the wine realm's unexpected delights and their power to evoke laughter, joy, and lasting memories. And to that end, perhaps wines should be evaluated not by their awards or pricing but by the happiness in each shared glass—a metric that would undeniably leave us all far richer than we ever imagined.

Discovering Your Grape Expectations: Approaching Wine Choices with a Smile

Life offers no shortage of mysteries: the origin of the universe, the meaning of consciousness, the criteria that determine the quality of a wine. Delving into the latter can be a daunting voyage to embark upon, one requiring resilience, a spirit of adventure, and most importantly, a dose of good humor.

So, how do we as intrepid explorers set off in search of our grape expectations? When approaching the world of wine, it is crucial to remember that there are no wrong answers, only varying degrees of personal preference. Every wine has a story to tell, and the beauty lies in finding those stories that resonate with our unique palates. As such, we must board the proverbial ship with no anchors, ready to glide across the wine ocean with an open heart, an open mind, and an open glass.

The first step in approaching wine choices with a smile is to suspend the notion that there are ironclad rules in the world of wine. While it is true that certain guidelines uphold the structure of this multi-colored mosaic of delights, we should never allow rigidity to stifle our curiosity and eagerness to experiment. In the words of the mischievous Dionysus himself, "Wine is beyond reason, an elixir of merriment and folly."

Sailing across the ever-changing waters of wine variety, we may encounter delectable Rieslings bursting with green apple sweetness, Chardonnays cloaked in regal barrels of oak, or Chenin Blancs offering the sweet caress of tropical fruit on our tongues. The delightful and confounding conundrum of wine is to find the profile that sings to our soul and invigorates our senses.

Imagine, if you will, being presented with a smorgasbord of grape varietals. The world's most brilliant sommeliers watch eagerly, awaiting your genius pronouncement of the perfect pairing for the rustic Coq au Vin before you. Observing the myriad choices, your mind flutters like the pages of a feverish novel, searching for the one wine that will unlock culinary nirvana.

But we should remember not to succumb to the pressure of the wine gods and goddesses watching from the pantheon above. Our liberation lies in embracing the mesmerizing spectrum of flavors and stories that wine has to offer, even the potential for an unexpected twist in the tale. Should we choose the ethereal delights of a Pinot Noir, or the peppery spice of a Syrah? To follow the serenade of the sommelier, or to venture into uncharted territory? The answer lies not in the expertise of the knowledgeable few but in the strength of our personal preferences.

Furthermore, it is important to remember that wine does not exist in a vacuum. Instead, the wine-soaked memories we cherish most often take place in the context of conviviality and camaraderie. A humble bottle of Chianti can be transformed into an unforgettable experience when shared with friends around a crackling fire, and a lonely sip of Champagne may never compare to the contagious laughter of a crowd. When discovering our grape expectations, we should be mindful of the environment in which we will be enjoying them, for it is the laughter and conversation that truly elevate wine into a transcendent experience.

Embarking on the journey to discover your grape expectations will undoubtedly lead to moments of comedy, calamity, and wonder. There will be the accidental discovery of a new favorite varietal, unbeknownst even to seasoned wine critics. There will be vigorous debate amongst friends over the subtle distinction between blackcurrant and blackberry on the palate of a Zinfandel. And there may even be the bittersweet realization that, despite its storied past, the fabled Pomerol may not be as rapturous as it is reputed to be.

Approaching wine choices with a smile allows us to tap into the joyful core of wine's essence, dispelling fears of inadequacy and replacing them with a profound appreciation for the myriad of stories contained within those glistening bottles. In this spirit of mirth and enthusiasm, our grape expectations will be revealed to us not with the clang of judgment but with the gentle embrace of a shared experience between friends, bound by laughter and love.

As we embark on our whimsical expedition across the landscapes of wine, let us remember the sage words of the great philosopher Voltaire: "Let us read, and let us dance; these two amusements will never do any harm to the world." And so too, through the boundless realms of viniculture, let us savor each sip, laugh with every mistake, and revel in the boundless joy and adventure that the world of wine so richly offers.

Tales from the Trolley: Rib-Tickling Wine Selection Mishaps and Victories

There are times in our lives when the universe rolls out the red carpet and bestows upon us moments of gloriously absurd humor, which we cherish as fond memories. The wine aisle, at times serpentine in its turnings and seemingly infinite in its provisions, is one such place where fateful encounters and bewildered musings can create rib-tickling tales of wine selection misadventures and victories.

Take, for example, the story of Carol, an aspiring sommelier, who found herself at her local supermarket one Friday evening, brimming with anticipation for the weekend ahead. She navigated the labyrinth of shelves with the precision of a cartographer, her gaze flitting between bottles of Cabernet Sauvignon and Malbec in pursuit of the perfect full-bodied red to accompany her homemade Bolognese. In her quest for optimal ripeness and tannin structure, she failed to account for one minor detail: the twin misfortunes of slippery fingers and gravity.

As the Bordeaux blend she had so carefully plucked from its perch slipped from her grasp, Carol watched in slow motion as the bottle shattered upon the unforgiving tiles, causing the rich, velvety liquid to pool around her feet. The resulting cacophony and stew of commiseration from fellow patrons was akin to a Greek chorus of lamentation, yet, amidst the chaos, a silver-haired gentleman emerged from the shadows, chuckling softly as he handed her a bottle of his favorite Malbec. Carol left the supermarket that fateful evening with a valuable lesson in humility, a newfound appreciation for Argentina's star varietal, and, perhaps most importantly, a wine-loving friend for life.

Then there is the tale of Stanley, a wine newbie wandering the grapevine-bordered aisles of his local market with a singular mission: to acquire a bottle of white wine for his dinner date with the captivating Eliza. Armed with the cryptic advice that "she likes Chardon-something," Stanley valiantly launched into the serried ranks of Sauvignon Blancs, Chenin Blancs, and Chardonnays. Like Theseus in the Cretan labyrinth, his resolve was challenged by the deceptive uniformity of colors and the complex lexicon of flavor attributes. Sifting through terms like "minerality," "oaky," and "buttery," Stanley's senses were flummoxed. Arriving upon a label describing the wine's profile as "zesty with a hint of summertime sadness," Stanley made the executive decision that it reminded him of Eliza's taste for both music and irony.

The evening arrived, and with it, anxious laughter and furtive glances filled the air as Eliza uncorked the Chardonnay with bated breath. The first sip was a symphony of citrus and tropical flavors, bursting like fireworks over a moonlit ocean. Stanley's gamble had paid off, and as he watched his enchanting date take another sip, he knew a victory of rare magnitude had been won. From that moment forward, Stanley vowed to never again underestimate the power of intuition and humor when it came to selecting wines.

And who could forget the saga of Bernadette, the taste-testing maverick who would sample the lip-smacking bounty of her market's weekly wine tastings with the finesse and curiosity of a culinary anthropologist? One sun-soaked Saturday afternoon, Bernadette weaved through the proliferating display of amber, ruby, and garnet-tinted bottles with her trademark confidence. As she reached for a taste of an Esoteric Gewürztraminer, she noticed her hand had been joined by another—a golden-haired woman by the name of Edith. An impromptu discussion of flavor undertones and curious anecdotes followed, as though Bacchus himself had declared them kindred spirits.

Their chance encounter led Bernadette and Edith to become partners in crime, embarking upon a rollicking series of vineyard visits, tasting forays, and bustling soirées that would have delighted even the gods themselves. And thus, Bernadette's wine shopping odyssey had yielded far more than a motley collection of bottles; it had borne the fruits of friendship and camaraderie that would echo across the rippling expanses of the grape harvest seasons to come.

These tales of heartwarming victories and worldly misadventures remind us that the wine aisle, much like the storied pages of history, is a treasure trove of humble and dramatic events that, when woven together, form the intricate tapestry of our lives. In navigating this enigmatic landscape, we rediscover the delightful unpredictability and the unyielding capacity for human connection that lies at the very essence of wine itself.

So, dear reader, take heed, and may the recollections of Carol, Stanley, and Bernadette serve as testaments to the kaleidoscope of inspiration and laughter that can be unveiled when one has the courage to venture between the grape-strewn shelves of wonder. For as the uilleann piper of legend once sang into the moonlit night, "Life is uncertain; drink the first glass in serenity, the second in anticipation, and the third in delight."

Winery Wonders: A Light-Hearted Expedition from Grape to Glass

Grape Hunting

As our mirthful foray into the enigmatic world of wine continues, we find ourselves at the hallowed gates of Vinelandia – the majestic and comical realm where raw green clusters of potential are transformed into the liquid gold we know, love, and occasionally spill on our unsuspecting friends. With a twinkle in our eye and a song in our heart, let us boldly embark on a light-hearted expedition from grape to glass, as we traipse through the highs and lows of the vinous creation process.

Imagine, if you will, the tousled-haired Bacchus striding through the dew-kissed vineyards on a sleepy summer morning, his rambunctious retinue of grape harvesters in tow. With the frenzied energy of a well-orchestrated comedic ballet, they scamper through the verdant rows of vines, plucking tender fruit with expert precision, pausing only to engage in the occasional grape toss or playful dance amongst the tangled branches. It is within this messy symphony of laughter and labor that the seed of wine's humor is first sown, sprouting tendrils of puns and wisecracks that will intertwine with the vine's very essence.

With baskets laden and spirits unfaltering, our convivial companions venture forth to the fermentation chambers – the mystical confines where the alchemy of yeast and sugar conspires to create intoxicating aromas of unbridled life. Within these bubbling cauldrons lie the beginnings of our wine's personality, blushing with delicate flirtations of fruit or brooding with the intrigue of savory secrets. As our bustling crew of grape harvesters toils away, chortling with each chaotic pour and splash, the tiny yeast cells join in the laughter, unceremoniously expelling alcohol and carbon dioxide as they cavort in their sweet, liquid playground.

But the journey through Vinelandia is far from over, for our vivacious would-be wine must now navigate the labyrinth of barrel aging. As the freshly-fermented grape concoctions embark upon their voyage into the oak vessels, navigating aromatic chambers filled with scents of clove and charred wood, an air of anticipation and mischief fills the winery. Like soothsayers peering into their crystal balls, the winemakers giggle and prognosticate over the flavors that dormant oak barrels may invoke, as they tease out unpredictable stories from within their wooden depths. Only time will tell what quixotic aromas and flavors the wine may gain from its barrel banter – a harmonious waltz of vanilla and spice, or perhaps a wild rumpus of smoky, savory notes.

Alas, the final rite of passage in our epic journey from grape to glass lies in the hallowed ritual of bottling, where a cacophony of clinks, clatters, and hearty guffaws echoes through the bustling assembly line. It is here that the true communion of wine with human mirth occurs – as if each tiny bubble of laughter from the critical bottling stage engenders the effervescent tingle we feel upon sipping the finished product. Through the whirlwind of caps, corks, and the occasional dash of chaos, our beloved wine is bestowed with its final vestments of labels, adorned with cheeky names and cryptic appellations that we, dear reader, will delight in unearthing as we peruse the aisles of our local wine emporium.

And so, having traversed the fanciful landscapes of grape harvest hijinks, whirlwind fermentation fandangos, and oak barrel capers, our heroic vintages emerge – sparkling with the wit and levity of their storied past. Whether it be a voluptuous red, brimming with the laughter of a thousand harvesters, or a sprightly white that pirouetted amongst the fermenting bubbles, each bottle tells the tale of its journey through Vinelandia with tongue firmly planted in cheek.

As we raise a glass to the misadventures and merriment that lie within each glistening bottle, let us remember the wise words of the Bard himself: "With mirth and laughter let old wrinkles come, and let my liver rather heat with wine than my heart cool with mortifying groans." For our wine is not only a testament to the diligent craft and artistry of winemaking but also a living archive of whimsy, imbued with the laughter, camaraderie, and yes, the occasional mishap, from its very inception.

In this rollicking landscape of absurdity and adventure, let us cherish the knowledge that every sip we savor is a dance with the wide-eyed spirits of the vine, who gambol amongst the hidden corners of Vinelandia, bridging the divide between nature and human folly with a hearty laugh and a raised glass.

Grape-Hunting Shenanigans: A Comical Overview of the Vineyard Harvest

Gather 'round, dear readers, for a bacchanalian tale like no other, as we embark on a journey to the source of wine's humor: the vineyard harvest. Yes, beneath the sun-drenched leaves and sinuous tendrils lies a rollicking playground of lively camaraderie and comical mishaps, a veritable breeding ground for grape-hunting shenanigans that punctuate the winemaking process with diligent labor and hearty laughter. Join us, as we bear witness to the raucous rites, uncanny exploits, and unbridled mirth of the harvesters who roam the vine-kissed hills, harvesting a potent amalgam of color, aroma, and anomaly.

In vino veritas, as the ancient adage goes, but in the vineyard, there is a truth of mirthful abundance, vibrant as the sunlit realms where plump, juicy orbs dangle from wisened vines. One can only imagine the juxtaposition of youthful exhilaration with this labyrinth of antiquity, giving rise to a kaleidoscope of vibrant emotions where skilled hands meet iron resolve, but also laughter, gaiety, and the occasional ill-conceived prank.

Take, for instance, the legend of Percival, a spirited initiate in the noble grape-picking fraternity, who in his eagerness to demonstrate his prowess, bit off more than he could chew on his first foray in the vineyard. Like a bespectacled Cyclops, he charged through the dense foliage with abandon, reaching for the most ripe and illustrious clusters that glittered promisingly amidst the sun-kissed flora. However, in his quest for perfection, our intrepid protagonist neglected to account for the cunning wisdom of Mother Nature, who, with knotted vines, led this spirited harvester into a trap too alluring to resist.

His foot entangled in a twisted mass of vines, poor Percival found himself suspended above the enchanting realm of his leafy conquests, upside down and vulnerable as his industrious band of winemaker comrades sauntered past, guffawing and clapping at the sight of his comical plight. It was there, in the sanctuary of foliage and laughter, that he learned his first lesson in the art of harvesting grapes: dexterity and resilience go hand in hand, but so do a hearty laugh and a nip of the ever-mischievous vine.

Equally memorable is the tale of the rambunctious collective known as the "Singing Harvesters," who in the crisp autumn air serenaded the vines and their fruit with songs of mirth and revelry. As their voices soared over the hills and valleys, their nimble hands plucking away at the grape bunches, they imbued the very fabric of their fruit with the spirit of song and life. They were a joyous cacophony of sound, laughter, and veritable vineyard merrymaking. Their belief that the vines and grapes would benefit from their heartening tunes may not have been scientifically founded, but their spirits were undoubtedly enriched by the harmonious marriage of wine culture and comical artistry.

Yet, what harvest would be complete without a mischievous interlude in the amaranthine sea of leaves and vines? I speak, of course, of the surreptitious grape toss, a time-honored tradition in the lore of grape-picking shenanigans. Armed with clusters of ruby and emerald orbs, the harvesters transform into impish warriors, engaged in a boisterous battle of wit and accuracy. With each well-aimed lob or fumbled catch, the air is filled with a blend of blithe laughter and the gentle tinkle of mischief, like Saturnalia in miniature. Indeed, the entire vineyard transforms into a starry-eyed playground of Dionysian delight.

From the audacious missteps of Percival to the harmonious antics of the Singing Harvesters, the anecdotes of comical vigneron exploits are a testimony to the indomitable spirit of vineyard workers and wine enthusiasts, who are blessed with the humility to laugh at themselves and the resilience to persevere through challenges. These moments of levity and connection, intertwined with the diligent labor of harvest, serve as a testament to the wonder and wit that permeates the very heart of the vineyard.

May we all, dear friends, learn from the mistakes of Percival, take inspiration from the harmonious sounds of the Singing Harvesters, and weave our laughter and gaiety into our work and pursuit of passion, as we venture forth into the expansive world of wine. After all, it is in the rhythm of the vineyard—the dance of the harvesters, the chorus of their laughter, and the rich tapestry of their uniquely human experiences—that we find the irrepressible essence of why we enjoy wine: to celebrate life and drink deeply from the chalice of camaraderie that unites us all.

High-Spirited Fermentation Follies: Transforming Juice into Liquid Gold

As we trace the vinous journey from vineyard to glass, our next adventure brings us to the rollicking realm of fermentation - a veritable alchemical playground, where the boundless energy of yeast and fruity elixir perform an intoxicating dance of transformation, conjuring forth the golden nectar we know and adore. Come, dear reader, as we descend into the bacchanalian frenzy of the fermentation chamber, peeling back the layers of this enigmatic metamorphosis to reveal the comedic twists and foibles that ensue as our beloved grape must assume its destined mantle as the elixir of life.

In the boisterous chaos of fermentation, we find a veritable cauldron of caprice, where the tireless work of tiny yeast soldiers, fueled by the sweet sustenance of sugar, excels in the protracted and jubilant battle of crafting our imbibable ambrosia. As they march through their realm, gobbling up each saccharine morsel, the yeast cells toil tirelessly, releasing the heavenly aromas and notes of ethanol that will lend our cherished beverage its mirthful essence. Indeed, the yeast-fueled symphony of fermentation is a cosmic dance of serendipity, as the frenzied communion of cells forges a riot of flavor from the primordial must, invoking the delicate infusion of fruit flavors and intricate aromas with bold strokes of gaiety.

However, at the core of this arcane alchemy, therein lies the humorous paradox of fermentation's finesse: the subtle art of controlled folly. It is the delicate balance between the exuberance of our microscopic yeast warriors and the watchful eye of the winemaker that coaxes forth the finest of flavors and delicate nuances of our destined draught. Picture, if you will, the furrowed brow of a vintner, billows of steam rising around her as she peers into the bubbling vat, clad in protective gear against the fermented onslaught, poised between the daring charge of the yeast and the cunning intricacies of her craft. It is a gentle comedy of errors, where the elusive sorcery of fermentation is forever poised on the precipice - a tipping point teetering between the triumphant symphony of crisp, ripe fruit and the jarring cacophony of unbridled funk.

In the labyrinth of fermentation follies, we meet our protagonist, the yeasty foot soldier, who traipses about his saccharine domain, fraternizing with his fellow cells, oftentimes with a rather acerbic wit. Our yeast hero, in his microscopic landscape, flits between the precarious strata of propriety and provocation, ever seeking the precise balance between chaos and harmony to bestow that divine humorous delight upon our palates, as we sip upon his bounty. Consider, if you will, the scenario of a yeast superhero - like an affluent knight, boasting a glorious cape of enzymes - embarking on his valiant mission to scour the depths of grape must, transmuting its base constituents with a flair for melodrama. It is a motley gallimaufry of fortitude and folly as our microscopic hero conquers grape after grape, manifesting his merry mead, all while seeking approval from his plucky companion, the winemaker.

Oh, the pressures that befall these tiny, wondrous beings, whose mission it is to bring forth the golden dew from their realm! The stage is set for a heated tango of tempers, as the compulsive desire for indulgence teeters on the cliff-edge of reason. It is in this precarious dance of the sublime and the absurd that one finds themselves ensnared in the complex comedic web we call fermentation.

And yet, as our tale draws to a close, we are left to ponder the bittersweet moral of our jesters' journey: that the creation of liquid gold is a labor of love, a serendipitous alliance between science and art, where the madcap capers of our microscopic heroes are harnessed by the deft hand of the vintner, who bestows upon each drop of elixir the warmth of their laughter, the precision of their skill, and the delicate imprint of their soul. Indeed, the quest for golden ambrosia is a boisterous emprise fraught with perils and pratfalls, but it is within the union of yeast and winemaker that we find the true essence of the winemaking process - the delicate mingling of chaos, love, and laughter in every glass.

What alchemy awaits, then, in the enigmatic world of barrels, as our freshly fermented concoctions seek illumined refinement amidst the shadows of the cellar? With bated breath and eager anticipation, let us venture forth into the darkened realm of the oaken vessel, a place where legends of whimsy and wisdom are forged, enthralling our minds and tantalizing our palates.

Barrel Buffoonery: The Amusing Art of Aging Wine in Wooden Barrels

As we delve deeper into the wine's beauteous metamorphosis, we arrive at the stage where our vinous nectar seeks the whispers of wisdom found within the staves of wooden barrels. These formidable vessels, brimming with both history and potential, cradle and cosset our treasured liquid, defining and refining its character with patience and wit. Come along, dear readers, as we traverse the hallowed halls of barrel-filled cellars, explore the complexities of the oaken union, and revel in the delightful absurdities that unfold in these shadowed sanctuaries.

Let us begin our journey into the realm of barrel buffoonery by acquainting ourselves with the leading character in this curious drama - the wooden barrel itself. A barrel is not merely a static tomb for imprisoned wine, but rather a dynamic partner in the winemaking process, adding depth, nuance, and intricate flavor through its complex web of attributes. Indeed, the barrel itself is no stodgy observer of the wine's metamorphosis but rather an effervescent maestro, directing the actions of its players through touch, smell, and taste. Picture, if you will, the barrel as an illustrious puppet master, garbed in the timeworn robes of its forebears, orchestrating the harmonies and complexities of its captive cast with a seasoned hand.

As the wine submits to the influence of the barrel, it undergoes a spectacular transformation in both aroma and structure, absorbing the essence of wood and exposure in a delicate dance of flavors. Here, dear readers, lies a tale ripe for comedic embellishment. In our magnificent theatre of the ironic and the absurd, imagine a cast of rowdy oak staves, each imbued with a distinct personality, partaking in raucous games of wine-infused charades beneath the cover of dusty cellar darkness. Each stave, armed with its own pedigree of ancestry and flavor, bestows upon the aging wine its unique contribution, painting an ever-changing canvas of vinous delight, swirled with strokes of spice, smoke, and, dare we say, shenanigans.

It is within the hushed confines of the cellar that our dashing duet, the wine and the barrel, unleash their comedic genius; a meticulous pas de deux of wit and wisdom, truth concealed beneath layers of irony and hyperbole. Consider, dear readers, the curious case of a particularly extravagant barrel, hewn from the most luminous wood of sun-drenched forests, ensconced in gleaming bands of gold. Within its gilded embrace lies a young wine, innocent and unassuming, timidly recoiling from the swagger and audacity of its resplendent host. With every sip, we imbibe the incandescent tension as it flares and ebbs between the wine and barrel, transported on a winding journey of self-discovery and comical intrigue.

Yet, in our spirited overture of barrel buffoonery, we encounter an underlying moral dilemma that permeates our tale, as we question the veracity and purity of our intrepid duo's partnership. Are we to celebrate unreservedly the delightful marriage of wine and barrel? Or shall we remain vigilant against overeager expressions of oaken influence, lest our once-bright beverage assume an impenetrable cloak of obscurity, rendering it a shadow of its former self? Such is the bittersweet tale of our enigmatic protagonists, forever locked in a cosmic pas de deux, seeking out harmony amidst the chaotic wonder of their curious world.

As we meander through the hallowed halls of the cellar, our minds filled with thoughts of rambunctious escapades, wine-soaked mysteries, and the gentle harmony of flavors, one can only wonder at the sequence of events that must follow for this bewitching libation to reach its highest potential. We have wandered the sunlit pathways of the vineyard, marveled at the frenzied energy of fermentation, and bore witness to the delicate dance of aging, yet there remains one final, crucial stage in the making of wine - the stage that seals the very fate of this noble exilir, ensuring that it traverses oceans and lands to find its rightful place among the pantheon of Bacchus' prolific creations: the act of bottling.

Let us eagerly venture forth, dear reader, as we approach the last leg of this oh-so-enchanting tale, a tale filled with anticipation, comedy, and skill, woven with the threads of ingenuity and boundless invention. It is in this final act that we bear witness to the unshakeable bond between varietal kin, as they courageously abandon the familiar comforts of their oak-ensconced haven, entrusting their ultimate fate to the vessel that will, ever so faithfully, transport them into the wide, awaiting world of wine enthusiasts and curious quaffers alike.

Bottling Bedlam: A Light-Hearted Guide to the Final Stage of Winemaking

Alas, dear reader, we have ventured down a winding path of viniculture, encountering a cavalcade of capers, misadventures, and behind-the-scenes tales of wine creation. We've peered into bubbling vats of fermenting frenzies, prowled the dusky corridors of barrel-occupied cellars, and reveled in the ribald humor that permeates these esoteric realms. Now, shall we delve into the final frontier of winemaking, in which all our efforts culminate in a symphony of capstones, closures, and capsules? Look, forsooth! The culmination of the quest awaits: the intriguing, confounding, and utterly essential process of bottling.

Before us lies a veritable wonderland of machinery and glass, a great mechanical Rube Goldberg of whirring conveyors and clanking contraptions poised to shepherd the exalted nectar into its ultimate vessel. We shall bear witness to the ceremonious and somber march of empty bottles, lined up with a zen-like poise and disciplined air, like soldiers on parade; their fate soon to converge with the vibrant, enigmatic concoction that courses through hoses, prepared to meet its destiny. Behold the ballet of the bottling line, a madcap display of confidence and timing, synchronized with a precision reminiscent of the finest Swiss watch: the twirling, the clapping, the swirling, the sealing; a symphony of cork, glass, and metallic contraptions, in a magnificent pas de deux of movement and mastery.

Within the vast expanse of this warehouse domain, there exists a realm of opportunity vast and expansive, for our cherished elixir to be played and finessed, as a virtuoso studies his instrument, eager to elevate the performance to the highest of highs. Does the bottle go elegant and seductive, swathed in a sultry silhouette and a cape of ripe color? Or does it opt for unabashed whimsy, encapsulated in a bottle embossed with fire-breathing dragons or resplendent superheroes? The comedic quandary of bottling finds its home amid this cavalcade of choices, and the wine in question now faces a test of identity, a veritable "choose your own adventure" of glassware and closure.

In this arena of closures, we find the epic stage of battle: an oft-contentious faceoff between the imperious cork, that familiar and reliable stalwart; and the young upstart, the ambitious and versatile screwcap. With furrowed brows and steely gazes, these opposing factions face one another, each poised to defend the honor of their chosen method - to the rapturous applause from onlooking wine aficionados and the bemused bewilderment of casual observers.

Picture the scene: a convention hall, packed to the rafters with enthusiasts and industry veterans, the tension palpable as each side vehemently extols the virtues of their hallowed closure of choice, whilst subtle and barbed mockery peppers their arguments like so many magenta strokes in a redolent glass of aged Syrah. This, my friends, is the comedic grappling of bottling - a spirited debate of functionality and frivolity, beguiling and all-encompassing, transcending the mundane and the everyday, elevating the process to the whirlwind heights of passion, witticism, and divine wit.

The journey, undertaken thus far, has been a riotous romp of delectable proportions: from the sun-dappled rows of vines, through the churning and tumultuous fermentation, to the otherworldly calm of slumbering vats, our passage through the annals of winemaking has been a sensory and cerebral delight. It is fitting, then, that we leave on a final note of observation, regarding the sometimes confounding, occasionally indignant, but always essential dance of bottling - a process that seals not only the fate of the wine but also the overarching tale of viniculture as a whole.

So, my friends, as the last resolute slurp of bottled ambrosia finds its way to our eager lips, accompanied by the unsettling gurgle that lingers long after the last glass has been drained, let us ponder the path traveled, the laughter shared, and the lessons learned. Gazing back at the marvelous panorama of winemaking folly, and forward to a future of well-advised forays into wine choice and enjoyment, we pause with solemn mirth at the cusp of our final frontier: bottling bedlam.

In our hands, we cradle the culmination of our cherished story, encapsulated in a vessel of glass, cork, and metallic grandeur. It stands at the ready, a loyal sentinel guarding our laughter and memories within a cloistered chamber filled to the brim with vinous brilliance. Let us clasp this reliquary, this time capsule of hilarity and human touch, and traverse the oceans and lands to bring it forth into our reverential circle, bestowing upon friends and strangers alike the gift of laughter, toasts, and lasting ties of community.

Wine Varieties: Laughing Our Way Through Labels

What's up with that label?

As we venture forth from the winery's enigmatic halls into the colorful kaleidoscope of consumerism, we encounter a realm populated with bottles of every hue, shape, and origin, beguiling in their quiet allure. Here, amidst the serried ranks of vinous grenadiers, humor and ingenuity engage in a spirited dance, as the tales spun on the surfaces of wine labels regale us with their wit, their wisdom, and their unabashed cheekiness. This infinitely diverse mosaic of vinous narratives is a veritable playground for those who revel in the union of the absurd and the profound, offering boundless opportunities for laughter and learning as we navigate the storied pathways of wine varieties.

Consider, for instance, the amusing game of balancing the varietal name's reputation with our expectations. Take, with a wink and a nod, the coy charms of the Viognier, a grape renowned for its seductive, sultry character. One can easily envision the naughty chortle of a winemaker as they craft a label that tantalizingly hints at the wine's voluptuous nature. With one eyebrow coyly raised, we can appreciate the allure of the label's imagery, knowing full well that it is but a playful hint at the wine's true essence, drawing us in like moths to the flame of Bacchus' all-knowing gaze.

Ah, but let us not neglect the sprightly charms of less celebrated grape varieties, who, with boundless spirit, confront tradition and popular opinion with a devil-may-care attitude, begging to be explored with a curious eye and giggling anticipation. The wine world's treasure trove of undiscovered labels offers a plethora of chuckle-inducing combinations, with monikers such as Pinotage, Gruner Veltliner, and Petit Verdot bemusing our tongues and tickling our senses as we dare to tear ourselves away from the comfortable familiarity of Chardonnays and Merlots. Much like encountering a rare and unusual creature in the wild, our explorations into these under-appreciated wine varieties can be as disconcerting as they are entertaining, as we tread the uncertain path through sniggers and bemusement.

In the vast expanse of the wine aisle, where multinational offerings jostle for our attention, the hallowed sacrament of terroir is elevated to a pedestal of comedic parody, as we witness the alchemical union of geography and grape variety unfold in often-humorous vignettes. From Argentine Malbecs donned in tango-attired dancers to South African Chenin Blancs adorned with sun-seeking lions, we can revel in the comic relief of caricature and whimsy, delighting in the knowledge that beneath the humorous veneer lies a foundation of love and passion for the land and its grapes.

Yet even within the confines of the wine aisle, where variety is embraced and celebrated, there exists a cadre of wine rebels, the nonconformists who choose to defy the norm and introduce unexpected wines into the mix, their labels resplendent with impish grins and tongue-in-cheek proclamations. It is in these iconoclastic offerings that our amusement reaches its zenith, as we discover bottles with names like "Strange Bru" (an unconventional red blend from Oregon) or "Bored Doe" (a whimsical take on Merlot from South Africa). The mirthful defiance of tradition displayed by these maverick winemakers can inspire us to take a second look, to question the infallibility of the all-knowing, or perhaps the all-deluding, Wine Guide, and to embrace the absurdity that arises from the knowledge that, sometimes, the best way to approach wine is to dance with it, not fear it.

As we meander through the eclectic landscape of wine varieties, our senses heightened by the prospect of uproarious encounters and beguiling revelations, we come to recognize that, in all its bewildering complexity, there exists a hidden thread of laughter and joy tying together our every wine-related endeavor. For it is in these delightful contradictions, where reverence for the grape meets gleeful irreverence, that we discover the true heart of wine lies not merely in its capacity to bring harmony and pleasure to our senses, but also in its potential to unite us all in the spirit of levity and laughter.

The images conjured upon lively labels, working in tandem with the absurd and oft-fantastical names, catapult us into a world where gods, monsters, and ordinary folk engage in humorous high jinks, united by the vine's transcendent power to metamorphose from humble grape to infinitely wondrous elixir. And so, lords, ladies, and scoundrels all: let us raise a toast to the infinite jest that is wine, and stride forth on a journey of mirthful discovery, in search of the witty, the whimsical, and the downright ridiculous in our quest to uncover the boundless treasure trove of laughter hidden within these vinous vessels, this vibrant tapestry of life contained within every bottle, every glass, every euphoric gulp.

Red Wine Riot: A Comical Trip Through the World of Red Wine Varieties

A tumultuous storm is brewing on the horizon, my esteemed companions, as we fasten our boots and don our umbrellas to embark on a riotous journey through the vine-tangled jungle of red wine varieties. No, there are no untamed vines seeking to drag us to the depths of intoxication abyss; rather, it is we who seek to plunge willingly into this vast, swirling soup of red wine history, bursting with amusing oddities, curious concoctions, and gargantuan grapes to amuse and delight both our minds and our palates.

Hearwwith, we begin our raucous red wine riot at the doors of the sumptuous Banquet Hall of Bordeaux, where the aristocrats of wine varieties nobly cavort in their stately minuet. Dazzling ruby-red gowns dance through the chamber as the lords of Cabernet Sauvignon lead the ladies of Merlot by the hand, their nimble dance steps skirting the salacious shores of crushing tannins whilst artfully avoiding a quick descent into the purple depths of inky, murky wines. Amid this grand cabaret, we pause with a chuckle for a side-eye glance at the boisterous antics of the mischievous Malbec, who, in a fit of rebellious energy, has cast off his Bordeaux shackles and darted off to Argentina, where he gleefully thrives among the pampas and the steaks, as he gamely gains fame with laughter in those fertile foothills.

Should we dare lax our attention in this dance of nobility, however, we may miss a fleeting glimpse of the Zinfandel beast, the shapeshifter who seamlessly sheds his European garb of Primitivo for the unabashed Americanism of the present day. Wearing his true guise, Zinfandel flaunts its wild swagger, cherry bomb explosions, and a touch of black pepper, with a mischievous guffaw that each gulp admits, corroborating its role as the perennial favorite at the wine-soaked barbeque feast.

As our rambunctious pilgrimage leads us through the winding streets of the winemaking city, we pause to join the thronging crowds gathered to witness the parade of the pinots—a march of anointed flavors from the grape's celestial inception to its earthly manifestations in the glass. From the pure, ethereal notes of a Burgundian Pinot Noir emanate sweet whispers of cherries and red currants, as devoted acolytes reverently bear garlands of violets and roses, and rose petals are scattered before the march's path. It is in the midst of this procession that we cannot help but feel a twinge of amusement as the merrymakers amble by, bearing flagons of new-world pinots, their irreverent flavors of raspberry, chocolate, and lusty earthiness boldly diffusing amongst the ether of the parade, poking fun at tradition and daring to bring forth innovation in the process.

Amid the bustling byways of the red wine realm, we discover a veritable tapestry of varietal curiosities that, in their own unique ways, offer settings for amusement in the most unexpected of places. We stumble upon the cheeky party that is Beaujolais, where Gamay grapes frolic in a madcap soiree, joyously expressing their ebullient cherry and cranberry delights in every sip. Around the corner, a surprising encounter awaits us with the carousing cluster of wild grape rogues, as they quaff resolute glasses of ruby-hued Syrah and Grenache, indulging in the revelry of smoky intrigue, white pepper, and tongue-tickling spicy encounters.

We alight upon a lively gathering bustling within a subterranean lair, where the disparate worlds of Tempranillo and Sangiovese collide in a mingling of smokey opulence and sun-ripened cherries all wrapped up in the firm yet amiable embrace of well-worn leather armchairs. Here we find both the laughter of a verdant Spanish taverna and the subtle humor of a rustic Tuscan osteria intermingling in the shared spaces between poetry and absurdity that are the wines' iconic flavors.

The red wine riot, with its ever-revolving cast of curious attendees, beseeches us to follow along as the kaleidoscope of flavors and aromas unfolds itself in a glorious cacophony of mirth, mayhem, and magic. It is these diverse threads of jest, jubilation, and the downright whimsical that weave into the rich, vinous fabric of memory and kinship that ties us together as we meander through the breathtaking world of red wine varieties.

White Wine Whimsy: A Light-hearted Exploration of White Wine Favorites

In a world often saturated with heaviness and sobriety, it is our delightful duty, dear reader, to embark upon a base-jumping leap of wit and fancy, directly into the effervescent fountain of hilarity that gushes forth from the robust world of white wines. Here, seated around a bubbling pool of companionship and joy, we shall journey through the hallowed doors of Chardonnay opulence to the whimsical grassy gardens of Sauvignon Blanc, unraveling secrets, spinning yarns, and uncovering the frolicking soul of merriment that lies deeply nestled within the heart of that most versatile libation—the blessed nectar of white wine.

As we set our course straight as an arrow of light towards the glistening halls of white wine variety splendor, let us first make acquaintance with the Chardonnay clan—the illustrious forebearers of the white wine world. Dwelling in the twin realms of Old and New, the Chardonnays possess a unique dexterity in adapting their flavor profiles to the whims of their winemakers with a sly wink and a playful grin. For in their homeland of Burgundy, glorious golden orbs of crystalline nectar emerge, exuding notes of toasted hazelnut, the soft aroma of rising brioche dough, and the velvety caress of a buttery vanilla silk. And yet, as their descendants spread forth to the sun-spangled landscapes of California, they transform with the agility of a pantomime artist, morphing their flavor repertoires to produce tastes of freshly peeled tangerine, the twinkling laughter of a pineapple sunburst, and the tender kiss of warm spice.

With exuberant joy, we tear our gaze away from the grandiosity of Chardonnay and prance with delight into the savory embrace of Sauvignon Blanc. Here, nestled within the pastoral splendor of rolling hills and grassy meadows, sauvy-b's flavors abound with the ripe zest of gooseberry and freshly squeezed citrus. The wine's inherent laughter, expressed in the unadulterated glee of its vivacious acidity, inspires amusing anecdotes as we regale one another with the legendary tangents of cat's pee on a gooseberry bush, a revered descriptor that elicits chuckles aplenty, as we bask in the collective glow of the witticism and the wine.

As we frolic from one lily pad of hilarity to the next in our romp through the white wine gardens, we cannot help but be mesmerized by the ethereal grace of Riesling, her filigree wings of mineral delicacy fluttering with gossamer lightness as she weaves her shimmering tapestry of sweetness and acidity. Nestled in the shadow of wind-swept mountains, and cradled in the embrace of steep vineyard slopes, Riesling's multifarious charms render even the most boorish and pompous wine critic prone to poetic fancies. With twinkling eyes, we witness the wine's audacious dance as it playfully skirts the precarious edge between honey's nectar and lemon's puckering pout, discovering in its pirouettes the essence of sweet laughter and the wisdom of balance on the precipice of life.

Though we could while away the hours swimming in the giddy rapture of the most globally adored white varietals, there lies a world beyond their plethoric charms, where the underdogs of the white wine domain frolic amongst the vines and the canopy, undeterred by their relative obscurity. As we take a turn off the beaten path, we stumble upon the Grüner Veltliner, a sprightly, spicy maiden of a grape that dances to the tunes of verdant effervescence. She dazzles our senses with the mind-bending enigma of white pepper and green apple, balanced precariously atop the slender blade of our perceptions, daring us to accept her playful challenge and unabashed defiance of convention.

Our trek through the wondrous, wit-laden landscape of white wines would be incomplete without a touch of the mysterious and the exotic. Swathed in the gauzy veil of enigma, the Viognier beckons us forth, her liquid gold luring us with the promise of the hidden delights. The wine, with a coquettish whisper, beckons us to peel back the layers of its character, revealing hints of apricot and luscious white florals. The sensual appeal of Viognier thrills our minds beneath the delicate orchestration of a wine that defies expectations, inviting us to partake in an intriguing tango.

And so we stand, fellow adventurers, amidst a glorious banquet of white wine wonders, alive with humor and mirth, intoxicated not only by the liquid contents of our glasses, but enchanted by the bacchanalian beauty of these merry elixirs that grace our lives with laughter and delight. As we sip upon the refreshing harmony of the flavors, let us also absorb the profound wisdom of the white grape's alchemical journey, recognizing the subtle dynamism of each sip as it shifts from levity to profundity. May we carry with us the spirit of these joyous grapes and the wry smiles they inspire as a testament to our indefatigable will to dance on the edge of life's duality, embodying the inimitable qualities of our cherished white wine allies: the perpetual pursuit of laughter and the exuberant embrace of hilarity in every drop.

Rosé Rendezvous: A Hilarious Guide to Tickled-Pink Wines

Ah, my dear friends, prepare to embark upon a delightful foray into the beguiling realm of finery fuchsia, where glass tints shift into hues more mystifying than a chameleon's chromatic capers, and where the whimsical world of laughter and levity finds its true origin in the blushing bosom of wine itself. Indeed, we can deny it no longer, as the bubbling effervescence of our excitement coalesces into a delightful eruption of hilarity—we are about to frolic through the pages of a story that unfolds within the shapeshifting shadows of the Pink Mystique, where the vats of vinous virtue meet their rosy counterpart in the guise of that most refreshing nectar—rosé wine.

Our rollicking adventure commences, fittingly, on the sun-drenched patio of a Mediterranean villa, where bronzed Adonis-like youth frolic among the bougainvillea, tossing up their wine-soaked locks in a playful game of Bacchanalian badminton, while the amused onlookers sip upon the delightfully humorous concoctions of rosé that so aptly mirror the splendid antics that surround them. Here, within the beating heart of the rosé motherland, we find the ancient vines of Grenache, Cinsault, and even that venerable libertine himself, Syrah, who doff their leafy caps to salute the sun's amber kiss, as they swell with a jovial blush of summertime joy.

Magnificent though the fruits of these traditional rosé vineyards may be, let us not tarry too long amidst the perfumed haze of nostalgia, for there are strange and beguiling elixirs to explore in the contemporary realm of rosé renditions. This, comrades in wine, is where our hilarious romp begins to unfold, as we chuckle at the cheeky audacity of the Australian white Zinfandel, a frivolous flirtation with the saccharine side of life, which tingles upon the tongue with the sweet seduction of a stolen strawberry kiss. As we are carried away on the wings of candied elation, we hear whispers of a chuckle borne from across the Atlantic, a musky mirth that emanates from the shores of California, where the blushing Pinot Noir seductively reveals its rosy underbelly in glasses that sparkle with the giggling glee of a thousand laughter-filled afternoons.

Let us now tiptoe past the gates of conventionality and plunge headlong into the delightful realm of the hilariously offbeat, the eccentric elegance that resides in the heart of Koshu, Japan's most revered grape for producing bewitchingly delicate rosé wines that play upon the palate like the lyrical grace of a thousand cherry blossoms aflutter in a gentle spring breeze. Steadfast in our pursuit of the fantastically absurd, we cannot help but pause to admire the cheeky joie de vivre of the orange-hued txakoli rosé from the Basque country of Spain, a tongue-tingling triumvirate of sprightly effervescence, whimsical acidity, and the playful prickle of a citrus kiss that tickles the furthest corners of our jollity.

As we swirl through the fascinating menagerie of rosé-driven laughter, we discover that the wine world's sense of humor lies not only within the glass but beyond it, in the ephemeral realm of those vinous vanguards who so delightfully dance to the beat of their own drum—and nowhere is this more apparent than in the zany, wonderful world of petillant naturel, or "pet-nat," wines. These bottles of bubbling froth and fun, often playfully referred to as the vinicultural equivalent of the unfinished novels of literature, are a living testament to the boundary-defying spirit of laughter in rosé wines. A sprightly combination of sass and fizz, the pet-nats of the rosé realm see themselves merrily fermented in the bottle, sealed with a crown cap, and poured into eager glasses with rightful pomp and ceremony, where they reveal themselves as mischievous sprites whose sparkle lies in their inexplicable allure as the unfinished symphony of wine.

Our rapturous exploration through the landscape of rosé rendezvous would not be complete without a nod to the grand dame of hilarity herself, that enigmatic entity that begets joy and laughter in every rosy sip: sparkling rosé. From the shimmering boudoir of Champagne, where the rosé sparklers exude sophistication in the form of wine glass ballets that dance between notes of wild strawberries and refined elegance, to the more boisterous bustle of Italy's Prosecco region, where the sprightly Brut and Extra-Brut rosés frolic like the court jesters of the vinous stage, this effervescent realm of tantalizing tints and playfully prickling bubbles represents the eternal, life-affirming laughter that unites us all in the shared bond of hilarious revelry.

Thus, we find ourselves, in this concluding blush of riotous reds and whimsical whites, perched upon the razor's edge of hilarity and profundity, where laughter meets wisdom in the embrace of that most pink of libations—the noble, tickling rosé wine. Let us then clink our glasses together in a toast to the unbridled joy and jocularity that is the soul of rosé, a symphony of shades and flavors whose notes reverberate through the echo chamber of vinous amusement, leaving traces of merriment upon every glass that brims with the blush of joy. As we clasp hands and raise our glasses to this splendid, wine-soaked adventure, let us remember that life, at its core, is a Dionysian dance of love and laughter—so let there be pink, let there be light, and let there be revelry in the ever-expanding realm of our rosé rendezvous.

The Eccentric Ensemble: Lesser-known, Yet Laugh-Inducing Wine Varieties

As we plunge into the buoyant waves of the eccentric ensemble, we are met with a chorus of whimsical characters whose lesser-known yet captivating charms tug at the corners of our smiles, inviting us to join them in a rapturous frolic through the vinous underbrush. From the mischievous glint of a Bacchus grape hiding coyly beneath the boughs of an English vine, to the roguish cackle of the Romanian Grasă de Cotnari, these lesser-known grape varieties reveal themselves as the motley crew of wine's mysterious backstage, their presence a tantalizing whiff of the hilarious yet undiscovered.

Our first encounter with this band of merry misfits is the enchanting Scheurebe, a beguiling grape from the heart of the

Germanic wine world that thrives on the steep hills and forest-shaded vineyards that line the banks of the river Rhine. A scion of Riesling's illustrious lineage, Scheurebe is a blend of regality and the mischievous, pairing the stately elegance of its parent with a sly, tongue-in-cheek twist on varietal expression. A glass of Scheurebe sparks a journey through a kaleidoscope of scents, from the audacious lure of blackcurrant leaf to the bold resonance of grapefruit zest, culminating in a crescendo of giggles with a playful virtuosity that tantalizes our senses with the promise of the unexpected.

We continue our expedition into the hidden corners of the wine world as we stumble upon the beckoning arms of the lesser-known yet utterly intriguing Furmint grape. A darling of Hungary's Tokaji wine region, Furmint is a captivating character in the tapestry of amusing wines. Draped in a cloak of mystery, Furmint navigates the treacherous dance between sugar and acidity, leaving wine aficionados breathless with anticipation as they ponder whether the wine they hold is a lusciously sweet or stunningly dry elixir. One cannot help but laugh at the absurd quandary presented to us by this delightful varietal, leading us towards a revelation that wine is not always a dichotomy of flavor, but rather, a celebration of the quirks and anomalies that render it a delightful source of amusement.

But of course, the eccentric ensemble would hardly be complete without the misfit prince himself—the beguiling

Rotgipfler, a rare Austrian grape that proudly bears the mantle of being a vinous wild card. Rumored to have been the wine of choice at Emperor Franz Joseph's imperial court, this intriguing varietal echoes with the laughter of ancient court jesters as it playfully traces a labyrinthine path between the lush, velvety richness of apricot jam and the bone-dry austerity of a desert landscape, coaxing a wry smile from the knowledgeable and the curious alike.

To think of the whimsical world of eccentric grape varieties without considering the effervescent charm of the Lambrusco family would indeed be a grave oversight. This featherlight, sparkling red wine variety is the unrivaled embodiment of Bacchus' playful laughter, as it bewitches the drinker's senses with a cascade of cherry, raspberry, and violet notes, all singing in harmonious revelry. Indeed, the Lambrusco is the court jester of wines—daring, surprising, and never quite what it seems.

The final destination of our animated adventure in the realm of lesser-known wines introduces us to the irresistibly cheeky Schioppettino, a captivating Italian grape that delights in turning the conventional wine world on its head. Hailing from the sun-soaked vineyards of Friuli, this bewitching varietal unfurls a slew of taste sensations that span the duality of tart pomegranate and heady black pepper, all underscored by a sprightly acidity that harmonizes the tongue into a gleeful tango. The Schioppettino grape is a message from the wine gods themselves, reminding us that life is indeed a lively, unexpected dance—so why not partake with laughter and mirth?

As we swivel away from this cavalcade of peculiar delights, we cannot help but feel a newfound appreciation for the mirthful magic that lies within the shadows of every hallowed wine cellar and vineyard walkway. The eccentric ensemble, with its incomparable blend of wit, intrigue, and unabashed originality, is a testament to the value of seeking out the surprising and the uncommon, of daring to venture forth from the well-trodden paths of the wine world and into the enigmatic arms of these lesser-known varietals. For as we've unraveled the laughter woven within the grapevine's yield, we see now that the eccentric ensemble serves as a mirror to ourselves—a reflection of the irrepressible spirit of hilarity that bubbles beneath the surface of even the most solemn of occasions, waiting only for the uncorking of a bottle, the clinking of a glass, and the inception of a new adventure amid the swirling effervescence of wine.

From Noble to Notorious: A Playful Peek into Celeb-Famous Wine Types

Gather round, my dear readers, as we set out on a ritzy romp through the glamorous vineyards owned by the very gods and goddesses of the modern age—celebrities. In this dazzling foray, we shall explore the whimsical intersections of fame, fortune, and vinification, unearthing the tantalizing tales that surround the world of celebrity wine-making.

Our journey into this sparkling realm begins, fittingly, upon the verdant slopes of Southern France's beloved Provence region, where the dashing Hollywood royalty and enviable power couple, Brad Pitt and Angelina Jolie, once shared their inspiring vision of viticulture. Behold the splendor of Château Miraval, a palatial estate that shelters a vineyard where the luscious Côtes de Provence Rosé wine is born. Indeed, this is a wine that echoes with the laughter of its creators—a beautiful ballet of pétillance and passion that unfolds within every glass and whispers to us the playful secrets of the stars that have tread upon these hallowed grounds.

Let us now venture across the pond to the rolling hills of California, where another cinematic icon has laid claim to a verdant vineyard that brings forth the fruits of hilarity. Within the idyllic confines of the Francis Ford Coppola Winery, we find a whimsical synergy of film and wine-making, as the legendary director himself expertly crafts a parade of delightful vintages that playfully wink at his storied filmography. From the tongue-in-cheek homage to his gangster epic in the form of a velvety "The Godfather" red blend, to the alluring ingénue of a white wine titled "Sofia"—named after his equally celebrated daughter—Coppola's vines intertwine with the annals of cinematic history in a playful dance between the grape and the silver screen.

As we continue our lighthearted exploration of celebrity-made libations, we find ourselves drawn to the illustrious gates of a vineyard imbued with the spirit of sporting triumph. Shafer Vineyards, owned by the esteemed baseball legend, Tom Seaver, is a tantalizing testament to the synergy between athletic prowess and the laughter of the wine gods. Gracing the Napa Valley with its enchanting presence, Shafer Vineyards boasts a glorious range of Cabernet Sauvignon wines whose rich, bold flavors speak of the tireless dedication and determination that have propelled both wine and sports to the heights of victory upon the global stage.

The charm of celebrity wine domains is not limited to the realm of the cinematic and athletic, for the bewitching allure of musical mirth finds its home among the vines as well. Comrade music enthusiasts, raise your glasses in salute to the wondrous Ignition Estate, a vineyard whose harmonious connection to the soulful tunes of the world-renowned musician, Sting, reverberates with every drop of wine produced. Here, nestled amongst the romantic hills of Tuscany, the dulcet notes of Sting's soul-shaking ballads intermingle with the intoxicating scents of the grapes, giving rise to a symphony of laughter and melody that enthralls the senses and elicits a chuckle from even the most stoic of hearts.

Our celestial journey through the vinous playgrounds of our modern-day Apollo and Dionysus figures would not be complete without a nod to the grand dame of hilarity herself, the illustrious television mogul who has taken the wine world by storm—Oprah Winfrey. Beneath the lofty peaks of Montecito's sprawling estates, the legendary television icon has crafted a delightful assemblage of wines that pay tribute to her life's work of spreading joy, laughter, and inspiration to the masses. Like the enigmatic goddess herself, Oprah's wines capture the essence of merriment and devotion, each refill an exclamation of exuberance, as if to say, "You get a glass! And you get a glass!"

As we draw the opulent curtain upon our kaleidoscopic tour of the celebrity wine phenomenon, we are left with the lingering sensation of laughter and wonderment that fills our souls with the joyful effervescence of life itself. The delightful union of fame, fortune, and vinification reminds us all that the true spirit of amusing wines resides not only within the glass but also in the hearts of those who dare to believe and achieve. So, my dear friends, let us fill our goblets with the mirthful elixirs of the stars and salute the hilarity that binds us all in a tapestry of intoxicating enchantment.

From the farthest reaches of the celestial vineyards to the hallowed halls of the Dionysian dance, we are all united in our common pursuit of joy, and it is within this shared bond that we discover the true essence of what it means to laugh, to love, and to live. So, to the celebrities who have so graciously opened their doors to the delights of the wine world, we raise our glasses in a toast to the hilarity that knows no bounds and echo their immortal words—cheers to laughter, cheers to life, and cheers to the soul of celebrity wines!

In Vino Veritas, In Humor Health: Closing Thoughts on Embracing Wine and Laughter

As our journey through the world of amusing wines and whimsical moments reaches its final act, we cannot help but pause and reflect upon the enduring bond between laughter and our cherished libations. This magical elixir, crafted from the earth's loving embrace and the tireless labor of those who transform humble grapes into works of art, serves as a conduit for connection and happiness. In vino veritas, we say, but we must also remember that in humor, we find a wealth of wellbeing.

Indeed, the synergy of wine and laughter is a potent force that transcends cultural, social, and geographic boundaries. We have traversed the tapestry of the wine world, from the bustling aisles of a busy supermarket to the verdant reaches of an isolated vineyard, seeking out those moments of hilarity that invoke our memories, anecdotes, and lively tales. These experiences remind us of the importance of looking at life through a playful lens, one that encourages us to appreciate the lighter side of a complex and often seemingly serious realm.

Wine has long been heralded as the essence of conviviality and celebration, a drink forged in the fires of Dionysian revelry and ancient Bacchanalian feasts. At the same time, laughter has held court as the inextinguishable flame that lights the human spirit, fanning the embers of togetherness, joy, and camaraderie when the weight of the world bears down upon us. As such, it seems only fitting that the two should intertwine, forming an everlasting partnership that speaks to the soul of our shared humanity.

For it is through the embrace of humor and the culture of wine that we are truly able to let down our inhibitions and luxuriate in the company of those who delight in the same idiosyncratic pleasures. Sharing in the unique nuances of a carefully crafted wine, paired with the thrill of lively discourse and spontaneous laughter, we find our spirits uplifted, our exhaustion eased, and our sense of purpose renewed. After all, wine is not merely a drink but an invitation to a sumptuous sanctuary where our bodies and minds may be refreshed and rejuvenated with the soothing balm of mirth and conviviality.

As we reconnect to our inner Bacchus, we realize that the key to maintaining a healthy relationship with wine is to approach it with a light-hearted air of curiosity, exploration, and most importantly, a surplus of laughter. By doing so, we liberate ourselves from the gnawing anxieties that plague the modern cellar dweller—the fear of making a faux pas, mispronouncing a wine term, or choosing the wrong vintage to pair with a Saturday night feast—and instead strike a balance that allows for the humorous mishaps to coexist with the elegance of our favorite libations.

In these final thoughts on embracing wine and laughter, let us not forget the gentle wisdom imparted by the poet Omar Khayyám in the tale of the Rubaiyat: "A book of verses underneath the bough, a jug of wine, a loaf of bread—and thou." This timeless reminder, to seek solace in the simple pleasures of companionship and laughter and to invoke the spirit of merriment that runs like a thread through the fabric of our lives, serves as an eternal testament to the importance of celebrating the joy and lightness that can be found in every sip of wine.

As we bid farewell to this whimsical journey and embark upon new adventures in the realm of wine and laughter, let us carry with us the lessons gleaned from these pages. For in the pursuit of happiness, we must remember that we are at once the navigators of our own destinies, and the explorers of life's most enchanting mysteries: the hidden treasures of friendship, the ephemeral beauty of laughter, and the pulsating heartbeat of human connection that echoes through the hallowed halls and laughter-filled cellars of the wine world.

In the spirit of vino veritas and the health of humor, dear reader, may your glass never run empty, your laughter never fade, and may your thirst for discovery remain unquenchable. For as we drink deep from the cup of life's merriment, we find our souls nourished by the nectar of joy, and our journey through the intoxicating landscape of wine and laughter becomes a path to serenity, savored one sip at a time.

Until we meet again, my fellow wine enthusiasts, let us raise our glasses and toast to the boundless laughter of the world, the effulgent light of humor, and the unparalleled richness of the inimitable wines that entice our senses and awaken our spirits, keeping us forever steeped in the joys of life itself. Salud!

Decoding Wine Labels with a Chuckle: Demystifying the Vino Vernacular

The output...or is the label right?

Ah, the wine label—a veritable canvas upon which the mysteries of the vinous world unfold in a dynamic tapestry of enthralling ambiguity. For many, the secrets of this scribbled parchment can prove as vexing as a Rubik's Cube and as inscrutable as the enigmatic smile worn by the Mona Lisa herself. Yet fear not, dear reader, for we shall embark on a whimsical quest to decipher the grape-inspired hieroglyphs and unlock the riddles that lie nestled within the silken folds of the cherished wine label.

As we wade into the inky depths of the wine label lingo, we are at once confronted with a panoply of enigmatic terms and phrases that beckon, confound, and beguile even the most intrepid of grape sleuths. Perhaps we spy the solitary term "Barrel Aged" emblazoned across the bottom corner surveying our confusion with an air of haughty disdain—barrel aged, you say? Why, a most Whisky-like notion, evoking wild images of burly oaken casks and the rhythmic tickle of the cooper's mallet. Yet in the vinous realm, this lofty title signifies a wine that has spent a portion of its life slumbering peacefully within the woody embrace of a carefully chosen oak barrel, absorbing its sturdy character and lending depth to the final elixir.

And what of the seductive allure of the twin words forever entwined in a dance of spirited merriment— "Appellation d'Origine Contrôlée"? Ah, here lies a straight-backed enigma whose stern countenance belies a rich, vibrant history as old as time itself. Hailing from the sun-dappled hills and verdant valleys of France, the Appellation d'Origine Contrôlée, or AOC, is the proud guardian of the noble traditions that have guided the country's storied wine industry for centuries, acting as a steadfast watchman that ensures each bottle bearing its regal seal meets the most exacting of standards.

As we pivot to the realm of New World wines, the label's linguistic landscape takes on a mischievous bent with the cheeky phrase "Contains Sulfites." The unsuspecting imbiber might recoil at the notion of consuming something so vaguely chemical-sounding—what sorcery is this? But, dear reader, let us not be disheartened. For the sulfites lie nestled within the bosom of nearly every bottle of wine that crosses our path, acting as a stalwart preservative that keeps the nectar fresh and vibrant, eschewing the specter of decay and the shadow of spoilage.

Our delightful foray into the vinous vernacular would not be complete without a cameo appearance from the star of the show—the ever-archaic and captivating "Residual Sugar." A phrase that sparkles with mischief, twisting the imagination into giggly imagery of mischievous sprites sprinkling granulated fairy dust upon row after row of hapless grapes. Yet these tantalizing words are simply code for the infinitesimal iota of sugar that remains within the wine after the mighty fermentation process has run its course, a whisper of sweetness that coyly dances a foxtrot with the bracing acidity and tannic structure of the wine itself.

With the incandescent purpose of the starry sky overhead, we turn our gaze towards the horizon and marvel at the sheer beauty of the vinous panorama that stretches before our eyes. The delightful delirium of unwrapping the veiled secrets embedded within the wine label has set our spirits aflutter and our hearts a-quiver. Together, we have traversed the glittering landscape of the wine label lexicon, unearthing the mischievous vernacular hidden within its elusive folds and emerging triumphant with a newly kindled passion for the spirited prose that pervades the magical realm of wine.

Vocabulary Vagaries: Hilariously Unearthing the Wine Label Lingo

Ah, the wine label—a veritable canvas upon which the mysteries of the vinous world unfold in a dynamic tapestry of enthralling ambiguity. For many, the secrets of this scribbled parchment can prove as vexing as a Rubik's Cube and as inscrutable as the enigmatic smile worn by the Mona Lisa herself. Yet fear not, dear reader, for we shall embark on a whimsical quest to decipher the grape-inspired hieroglyphs and unlock the riddles that lie nestled within the silken folds of the cherished wine label.

As we wade into the inky depths of the wine label lingo, we are at once confronted with a panoply of enigmatic terms and phrases that beckon, confound, and beguile even the most intrepid of grape sleuths. Perhaps we spy the solitary term "Barrel Aged" emblazoned across the bottom corner surveying our confusion with an air of haughty disdain—barrel aged, you say? Why, a most Whisky-like notion, evoking wild images of burly oaken casks and the rhythmic tickle of the cooper's mallet. Yet in the vinous realm, this lofty title signifies a wine that has spent a portion of its life slumbering peacefully within the woody embrace of a carefully chosen oak barrel, absorbing its sturdy character and lending depth to the final elixir.

And what of the seductive allure of the twin words forever entwined in a dance of spirited merriment— "Appellation d'Origine Contrôlée"? Ah, here lies a straight-backed enigma whose stern countenance belies a rich, vibrant history as old as time itself. Hailing from the sun-dappled hills and verdant valleys of France, the Appellation d'Origine Contrôlée, or AOC, is the proud guardian of the noble traditions that have guided the country's storied wine industry for centuries, acting as a steadfast watchman that ensures each bottle bearing its regal seal meets the most exacting of standards.

As we pivot to the realm of New World wines, the label's linguistic landscape takes on a mischievous bent with the cheeky phrase "Contains Sulfites." The unsuspecting imbiber might recoil at the notion of consuming something so vaguely chemical-sounding—what sorcery is this? But, dear reader, let us not be disheartened. For the sulfites lie nestled within the bosom of nearly every bottle of wine that crosses our path, acting as a stalwart preservative that keeps the nectar fresh and vibrant, eschewing the specter of decay and the shadow of spoilage.

Our delightful foray into the vinous vernacular would not be complete without a cameo appearance from the star of the show—the ever-archaic and captivating "Residual Sugar." A phrase that sparkles with mischief, twisting the imagination into giggly imagery of mischievous sprites sprinkling granulated fairy dust upon row after row of hapless grapes. Yet these tantalizing words are simply code for the infinitesimal iota of sugar that remains within the wine after the mighty fermentation process has run its course, a whisper of sweetness that coyly dances a foxtrot with the bracing acidity and tannic structure of the wine itself.

With the incandescent purpose of the starry sky overhead, we turn our gaze towards the horizon and marvel at the sheer beauty of the vinous panorama that stretches before our eyes. The delightful delirium of unwrapping the veiled secrets embedded within the wine label has set our spirits aflutter and our hearts a-quiver. Together, we have traversed the glittering landscape of the wine label lexicon, unearthing the mischievous vernacular hidden within its elusive folds and emerging triumphant with a newly kindled passion for the spirited prose that pervades the magical realm of wine.

Lingering beneath the surface of the wine label's esoteric enigma lies a hidden trove of laughter and enlightenment, a secret wellspring threaded with strands of humor and wisdom as complex and enchanting as the vinous tapestry adorning our glasses. By unlocking the door to this cherished realm and stepping over its hallowed threshold, we are granted safe passage into a land where laughter bubbles up like the finest effervescence and mirth pours forth with the robust vitality of a full-bodied red. With our trusty lexicon in hand and an impassioned heart, we depart from the coastline of the wine label's Vocabulary Vagaries to embark upon a bold new journey through its enchanting realm, exploring the uncharted territories of Geographic Giggles and braving the sharp-edged wit of Bizarre Blends. And so, dear reader, let us take up our corkscrews and conspire to shake the very foundations of the wine world, laughing and cavorting as we journey towards the veritable treasure trove of vinous adventure that lies shimmering like a siren call just beyond the horizon.

Geographic Giggles: Deciphering Wine Labels Across the Globe

Ah, the tantalizing tapestry of the wine label—a veritable microcosm of the terrestrial bestiary, as diverse and eclectic as the many vinous delights that slosh and pirouette within their glassy confines. From the lofty slopes of French vineyards to the sun-soaked Australian bushveld, each label betrays a multitude of secret codes and hidden machinations which, when unlocked, offer a vibrant portrait of the liquid symphony that lies nestled within the confines of its husky crystal chrysalis.

As we embark upon our geographical gallivant into the depths of this resplendent world, we find ourselves swept up in a whirling dervish of linguistic flotsam and jetsam that buffets our consciousness with the force of a titanic typhoon. Yet the intrepid wine warrior must not allow this tumultuous sea of lexical waves to dash their spirits upon the jagged rocks of despair. Instead, we must hoist the flag of our curiosity high into the air, arm ourselves with the compass of fortitude, and set a course through the seductive eddies of language and culture.

Let us start our whimsical journey on the shores of the Old World, where the vineyards of Europe cling desperately to their ancient soils, warding off the encroaching tendrils of modernity and progress with resolute ferocity. In the green and verdant heartlands of France, the wine label takes on a distinctly regal air, bestowing upon its oft-confounded audience a litany of noble soubriquets and appellations that hint at a lineage as old as time itself. Here, the wines are often named for the regions in which they're born, leaving one bemused by the interlocked vowels and subtle consonants of terroir-tastic terms such as "Bourgogne" and "Sancerre" and charmingly confounded by the omnipresent AOC assault.

In sublime Italy, the situation grows yet more perfidious, as the labels erupt in a cacophony of cacophonous names that bear testament to the illustrious history of this blessed land. Fear not, dear gastronome, as the answers to these riddles lie curled within the sensuous arms of geography. Know that "Barolo" and "Barbaresco" pirouette upon the vine-strewn terraces of Piedmont, while "Amarone" and "Valpolicella" clamber among the gentle hills of the Veneto. Delve into the depths of wine Dante, and emerge triumphant with a sonnet to the sublime liquid spheres contained within.

As we trace a serpentine path across the wine-rich landscape, we arrive at the sun-kissed strands of Australia, where the New World's linguistic landscape acquires a distinctly mischievous air. Here, what was once obfuscated in the Old World becomes transparent with a twist. No longer must we decipher the whims of terroir and vintage; instead, the flow of information concerning grape variety, alcohol content, and producer is laid bare for all to ponder and peruse. With the irreverence of a bounding kangaroo, wine labels dance across the Outback, telling bold tales of "Shiraz" and "Chardonnay," with nary a nod to antiquated rules or stuffy bureaucracy.

As we draw the dusky cloak of our wine-soaked adventure around our grateful shoulders, be it with bewilderment, wonder, and horror, one cannot help but marvel at the dazzling menagerie of language and culture that bedecks the vinous landscape. Indeed, the wine label has revealed itself to be a tantalizing mosaic of stories, secrets, and mysteries that are bound only by the fertile roots that birth their liquid progeny.

From the fragrant French vineyards to the towering cliffs of Spain, to the rolling hills of Italy, and beyond, the wine label stands sentinel, an ever-present codex which, once deciphered and unfurled like a well-worn map, unveils the storied journey that brought the liquid treasure of our glasses to life. As we drain our sparkling vessels and lay our weary minds to rest, let us revel in the whispered secrets shared across the miles and celebrate the unparalleled diversity of our vivacious vinous crew. For in these myriad tales of geographical dalliance, we discover the variegated tapestry of human endeavor, a testament to the fortitude and ingenuity of those who dare to tame the vine and extract its liquid essence. We drink to their devotion, and in doing so, we celebrate the cherished riddle of the wine label—a geographical giggle for the ages.

Glassy Graphics: Quirky and Confusing Labels that Make Us Smile

An argosy of bewitching imagery and colorful language sets sail upon the tempest-tossed waters of our venerable wine labels. Their vibrant panoramas draw us into an intoxicating tableau that parallels the myriad nuances of the vinous nectar they cradle within their glassy embrace. From fiercely-elaborate designs, confounding typography, and enigmatic illustrations, wine labels teeter on a delicate balance between art and information, leaving us, the professed tipplers, wondering what secrets lie beneath their comical façades.

As we navigate the twisting, winding journey through the supermarket aisle, we encounter peculiar labels that instantly capture our attention with their curious graphics, challenging us to decipher the encrypted tango that dances before our bemused eyes. A plump, crimson rooster presides over a wild garden, his crimson plumage peppered with the shimmering vestments of fallen stars; does his proud crow bode well for the organic Red Rooster Cabernet within? Then, there is the svelte black cat, its emerald eyes glittering enigmatically against a backdrop of burnished gold, an ode to the velvety cat's purr of the Pinot Noir it vaunts.

Herein lies the cryptic allure that is the label's artistic realm, a dreamscape of symbols and allegories that poses the eternal conundrum—do they tease us with their frivolity, or are they innocent bystanders, caught up in the swirling maelstrom of vinous mythology?

As we delve deeper into this intoxicating narrative, a staggering trifecta of glassy kinetics springs forth with the gusto of a Bacchanalian harvest—pyrotechnics that test the very limits of our mortal understanding. From the inky depths of the Malbec, a frolicsome octopus unfurls its sinewy tendrils, an ardent gesture of passion, tenderly embracing a wayward whale—what seafaring secrets do these gentle giants whisper as they vanish into the purple abyss? And what of the surrealistic parade, a cavalcade of grinning jackalopes that leap, hurling themselves towards an indomitable crescent moon, invigorated by the sprightly Syrah they champion? Surely, there is a message here, a playful riddle from the vineyards to tease our mortal desires.

Then, our weary gaze alights upon a magnificent panorama that awakens a delicious, intriguing thrill deep within our souls—a diorama that is at once whimsical and yet suffused with the inimitable spirit of human triumph. The interstellar saga that unfolds across the parchment of Cabernet Sauvignon—a rattling skeleton riding an indigo rocket ship, embarking upon an endless quest through the inky infinity, her laughter ringing out like the peal of a cosmic bell. The truth we seek, perhaps, lies somewhere in this cosmic spectacle: a revelation that, as we hurtle through the unknown, we carry with us the memory of countless lifetimes stored within the very essence of the wine—each glass a microcosm of laughter, tears, and unrelenting humanity.

As we emerge from the depths of our glassy wanderings, gasping for breath and blinking away the intoxicating reverie that has enthralled our senses, we cannot help but marvel at the perplexing nexus that lies at the very heart of our wine labels' bewildering semantics—a swirling maelstrom of conundrums and enigmas, as incomprehensible as the haunting siren song of the celestial void. Here, in this frenetic realm of boundless imagination, we stand poised to unravel the intricacies of a universe that teases us with its infinite possibilities and unrestrained laughter.

The fleeting moments of recognition, of finding ourselves irresistibly drawn into this world of glassy myth and legend, allow us to steal a captivating glimpse of the shimmering prism that is the human experience—illuminating the boundless potential of our palates to appreciate both the aesthetic and flavorful tapestry that makes up the incomparable universe of wine. For with every comical misinterpretation we encounter, and with each quirky adventure we embark upon, we forge an ever-lasting bond to the vinous landscape that nourishes the soul, and in doing so, we nourish our penchant for vivacity, for laughter, and for life.

With a snifter of whimsy and comical resolve, we unfurl our lips into grins that stretch from one side of the supermarket aisle to the other. We raise our glasses high, a raucous toast to the tongue-in-cheek chimeras and cryptic alchemists who haunt the giddy peripheries of our imagination. We drink to their foibles, and in doing so, we celebrate the eternal conflation of art and enigma that is the glorious, multifaceted jungle of our wine labels—a realm where laughter and understanding intertwine, and where we beckon the roar of a scarlet lion or the cackle of the golden rooster to guide us through the swirling maze of our wildest dreams.

Bizarre Blends: Funny Wine Names and Their Origins

Far be it from the realms of dry, stuffy academia, or the silent, well-groomed halls of high society, for here we shall delve deep into the glassy grottos of alcoholic ambrosia, where we will mine the subterranean lode of whimsy and levity that threads its way into the colorful tapestry of vinous lore. And like a geological gumshoe, we shall plumb the fathomless depths—not of the wine glasses themselves, nor the blend that dances within, but of the light-hearted nomenclature that festoons the world of wine making with the wink of a maiden's eye, the quirk of a mustachioed smile, and the occasional, triumphant, if slightly inebriated, leonine roar.

As we embark upon this riotous roller coaster of wild lexilogical wonders, the wine list unfurls before us like a vermilion parchment, revealing the names of many a fine vintage, each one a treasure trove of mispronunciations, ribald double entendres, and seemingly ridiculous claims, all conspiring to carve a grin upon the once-stoic face of its hardy consumer.

Who amongst us could fail to stifle a chuckle at the mention of the robust Australian "Curly Flat," a varietal with a nom de plume that is at once lively and outrageous? Or the effervescent "you-know-what I mean," an adjective-laden Californian Cabernet Sauvignon that leaps into one's mind-cellar with the impishness of a grammar-loving hobgoblin?

Surely, these could not be mere accidents, but rather the deliberate machinations of some wise, wry, and winking spirit that embraces the very essence of the vinous lexicon, with one foot planted firmly in the soil of humor.

As we traverse the hills and valleys of this wacky wine atlas, we encounter yet more examples of bizarre blends and their fantastic, laugh-inducing origins—a testament to the creative powers of their creators in concocting not just the liquid lightning in the bottle, but the very names themselves that effervesce upon our lips with a frothy chuckle.

Take, for instance, the "Cardboardeaux," a paradoxical paradox of a blend that invites you to ponder the interplay between a presumably fine Bordeaux and the ignoble reputation of boxed wine. Surely, you must wonder, the tongue that dances across the rim of such a peculiar vessel would come away both lifted by the exquisite sensation of the wine, and yet smiling at the outrageousness of the label that has been its chaperone?

We must not forget the equally intriguing, and even more brazenly puerile, "Fat Bastard," a wonderfully jowled and mischievous moniker that hails from the land of egalité and libérté. Dare we say that entrenched amongst the august vineyards of France, such irreverent effrontery is borne not of disdain for tradition, but a spirited nod towards the unfettered millennial whimsy that threatens, at every turn, to topple millennia-old enigmas and antiquated appellations?

Indeed, the world of the bizarre blends hints at a vinous revolution, led by the wine labels that dare to flaunt their insouciance, their esoteric humor, and their riotous titillation right there, upon their bold and brazen faces—an army of rogue rascals standing defiantly in the face of oenology's stodgy status quo.

Yet we must not forget those blends that harbor within themselves a more subtle comic vein, their origins garbed in the cloak of history or ancient lore. Consider the whimsical, centuries-old tale of the South African blend "Goats do Roam." This mirth-inducing moniker hearkens to ancient Rome's amphitheater playground, its bolshy, bleating protagonists given free rein to butt against hapless gladiators, their rutting antics played out to the riotous roars of amused spectators.

Throughout our glassy journey of discovery, we bear witness to the origins of countless curious blends that infuse the world of wine with their own effervescent energy, a luminous mirth sparked in the laughter that bubbles up with each teasing sip. As we tip our glasses in salute to the eternal hilarity of wine names, we embrace the playful, the clever, and the downright silly, escalating even the humblest drop of grapey goodness into an elixir of eternal levity and joy.

Vintage Vino: Cracking the Code on Wine Age with Laughter

In the sparkling cosmos of vinous constellations, spotting the glorious glimmers of a vintage vino is akin to decoding the arcane navigational maps of ancient mariners. Drawn to the magnetic allure of these celestial orbs, we traverse the murky depths of our wine glasses with bated breath, guided by the siren song that lures us to the shores of laughter and delight. As we embark on this thrilling odyssey through the rarefied realm of aged wine, we cannot help but ponder on the comical capers that ensue whilst we grapple with the enigmatic mysteries of the eons in a glass.

Picture, if you will, the harried oenophile who fumbles and fidgets their way through the labyrinth of dusty cellar aisles, a determined glint in their eye and an iron resolve to excavate a time-treasured gem. Yet, they are not alone on this quirky quest. Each of them is shadowed by a silent presence, a wry, bemused specter that regards their frantic foraging with a raised eyebrow and a smug smile. This ethereal guide, our light-hearted, laughter-tipped mentor, seeks to reveal the oft-hidden comic vein that permeates the Wine Age Arcanum - a repository of jocularity, hilarity, and down-right tomfoolery.

For who could not let out a guffaw when confronted with the farcical tale of an esteemed Cabernet Sauvignon, cradled lovingly in the depths of a crypt-like cellar for decades, only to awaken from its vinous slumber like a veritable Rip Van

Winkle, wrathful and roaring with the indignation of a thousand screaming hangovers? Is there not an element of slapstick humor in the somber pursuit of the elusive treasure trove of a fine vintage, as we fumble and bumble our way through the dusty catacombs of wine history?

Yet, the eternal irony of our spirited quest through the fog-enshrouded mists of wine-age mirrors the inevitable folly and fallibility of human nature. For as we cling to the dazzling brilliance of a perfectly aged Grand Cru, its liquid history intoxicating our senses with a delightful frisson, we often overlook the gentle chuckles that bubble beneath the surface. The subtle reminiscences of comical misadventures, the anecdotes of tipped glasses and spilled decanters, and the whispered hiccups of evening secrets long since forgotten.

And, as we gaze into the swirling depths of an amber-hued Sauternes - its golden age marking it akin to the lustrous sands of an hourglass - we find ourselves in the throes of a transcendent revelation, a symphony of laughter that echoes through the cavernous reaches of our souls.

In these hallowed reveries, we encounter the caustic wit of a vintage Port, its tannic piquancy tempered by decades of careful aging, now bursting forth with a sardonic chuckle reminiscent of a time-worn uncle, his wink as audacious as it is endearing. Or consider the ethereal Riesling - aged as gracefully as a porcelain-skinned maiden, its delicate complexity now infused with a light-hearted hilarity that teases the edges of our palates like the wistful lilt of a summer breeze.

These mischievous encounters with the spirited elixirs of vintage wines only serve to underscore our own inexorable march towards the dusty shores of time. And yet, in doing so, our hearts and palates are imbued with an irrepressible lightness, an intoxicating buoyancy that derives from our ability to laugh into the abyss with the reckless exuberance of a starry-eyed sailor.

As we raise a glass to our enigmatic phantom guide, our laughter cascading through the sepulchral cellar as we toast to the joys and wonders of a wine well-aged, we come to realize the eternal truth, the sparkling nugget of wisdom that lies at the very core of our wine-age escapades: that, in every bottle of vintage vino, there dwells the inimitable spirit of laughter, a celestial delight that transcends the chimerical boundaries of time and space.

So, dear tipplers and bibulous brethren, let us voyage onwards into the realm of future hilarity, guided by the whispered laughter of bygone ages and inspired by the comical capers that lie in wait within every well-aged bottle. Let us clasp the hand of levity and mirth as we wade into the mystic depths of the epochs in a glass, unlocking with every sip the boundless potential of our laughter-infused hearts. And let us sail into the boundless cosmos of vintage vino, armed with laughter and fortified by the celestial radiance of the vinous stars.

Alc Abundance: The Comical Side of Alcohol Percentages on Labels

As our odyssey through the whimsical world of wine continues, we find ourselves peering intently at the line of numbers and letters that adorn their glassy surfaces. As our eyes flit past the perennial enigmas of appellations, grape varieties, vintage dates, and oddball names, our focus narrows to the tidy row of digits that declare, with all the solemnity of a court jester's proclamation, the hallowed percentage of alcohol by volume (ABV).

Ah, the curious world of alcohol percentages, a realm of mirth and mischief that embodies the very spirit of exhilarating inebriation and misadventures awaiting within the confines of each corked and bottled vessel. There, etched upon the label by some numerical nymph or perhaps a mathematical maestro, oftentimes lies a delightful tale that titillates with a wink or a sudden comedic burp, a tale that subtly reveals the inherent potency of the libation contained within.

For how could one not be charmed by the balletic pas de deux of numbers dancing a delicate dance upon the label of a Moulin-a-Vent, its 13.5% ABV declaring its robust character with a poetic flourish? The revelers imbued with a healthy measure of this mercurial elixir are taken by storm, their minds abuzz with dulcet laughter and hearts aflame with a sudden ebullience. There is a cheekiness to this serendipitous number, an impishness that beckons the taster to engage in a lilting, high-gravity waltz that echoes the idiosyncratic terroir from which the wine hails.

And then there are the quixotic, seemingly arbitrary percentages of alcohol that dance atop the labels of some wines, their curious notations insinuating a witty narrative that is at once puzzling and amusing. Picture, for instance, an impetuous Sauvignon Blanc skyrocketing to a stratospheric 14.79% ABV—who could have surmised that such a seemingly innocent libation would harbor an unbridled penchant for high-octane hijinks? Or even the whimsical musings of a 12.34% Valpolicella Ripasso, whose seemingly capricious figures defy conventional wisdom and invite us to partake in its spirited story with a raised eyebrow and a chuckle?

It would be remiss of us, however, not to acknowledge that there exists within the world of alcohol percentages a certain risk for inadvertent impropriety, a vulnerability to the wild machinations of those mathematical pranksters whom we adore. How often have we been beguiled by the clever juxtaposition of two unassuming numbers, the conspiratorial duo of 6.9% or 7.1% declaring their presence with a barely suppressed snicker? Indeed, even amongst these somewhat disheveled ranks, the potential for levity emerges in the most unexpected of places.

Yet the wit and whimsy of alcohol percentages do not merely reside in the numerical realm, oh no. A veritable menagerie of absurdist names, titles, and labels await those brave drinkers who dare to traverse the hazy boundary between sober propriety and tipsy titillation. Of course, we are referring to those bold and audacious producers who have gleefully embraced the inherent levity of high-alcohol wines, bestowing upon their potent potions such delightful monikers as "The 16% Solution" or "The Histrionic Howler," their tongues firmly planted in cheek as they pay homage to their concoctions' boozy boisterousness.

This delightful tapestry of comical alcohol percentages and fantastical names serves to remind us that wine, at its very essence, is a liquid art form that has the power to marry the mundane with the sublime, to elevate the pedestrian act of deciphering a simple string of digits to an enraptured, laughter-infused reverie. And so, as we raise our glasses in salute to the playful caprices of alcohol percentages, let us embrace the spark of joy and jest that springs forth from the unlikeliest of places.

Indeed, in the murky depths of each delectable glassful of wine, there spends a vast constellation of laughter just waiting to be unlocked and unleashed. So, let us raise our glasses and toast to the eternal sunshine that resides within our hearts, boundless and bubbling with mirth, as we navigate the rippling ocean of whimsy that is the comical side of alcohol percentages on labels. Let the intoxicating, effervescent spirit of humor be our saving grace as we plunge deeper into the world of wine, buoyed by the ceaseless tides of laughter and delight that carry us ever forward.

Taste Ticklers: Humorous Interpretations of Wine Descriptors

As we stride forth on our journey through the whimsical world of wine, we are met with a myriad of delicious and perplexing descriptors - words and phrases that attempt to capture the essence and character of each unique and intoxicating vintage. These swirling kaleidoscopes of language, much like the wines they aim to reveal, often inspire chuckles, confusion, and bemused delight. Join us, then, on an exploration into the peculiar universe of wine-speak, where we shall sip and savor our way through the outrageous, fantastical, and downright bizarre language of wine.

Take, for instance, the humble "wine-y" descriptor. A comical paradox in its sheer simplicity. Why not describe a glass of wine as "wine-y," after all, is that not what it is? Yet, the uninitiated among us might scoff and chuckle, imaging a winemaker or sommelier as some kind of jester in grape-stained garb, gleefully branding their bottles with a smug, knowing grin. Little do they know that this seemingly nonsensical term is actually an entirely legitimate descriptor, referring to the secondary fermentative aroma characteristics of a glass of wine.

Or consider the playful and slightly bewildering term "unctuous." Perhaps most commonly associated with a duplicitous or insincere individual, the thought of a wine embodying such traits is at once hilarious and befuddling. Yet, to the discerning and experienced palate, an unctuous wine simply refers to a velvety and rich texture, with a mouthfeel that lingers long after the liquid has disappeared.

Certainly, one cannot help but giggle when confronted with the fanciful notion of a "vegetal" wine. Are we to expect our humble Bordeaux to sprout brassica-esque limbs and wander the aisles of our local supermarket produce section? Perhaps not. And yet, the world of wine is filled with verdant and herbaceous expressions - the wafting scent of bell peppers in a glass of Cabernet Franc or the asparagus-like aromas in a Sauvignon Blanc. In these bottles, we catch a glimpse of nature's playful wit, expressed through her vinous creations.

And let us not forget the delightful confusion inspired by the elusive and mysterious descriptor of "minerality." Often intertwined with the mythos surrounding terroir, the concept of minerality in wine inspires debate, bemusement, and comedy in equal measure. Is the loamy, gravel-like scent detected in a Rioja a nod to the soil from which the Tempranillo grapes sprung? Or is it mere poetic fancy, the perceptions of a wine-drinker eager to find a connection between glass and earth? Regardless, the term has become a go-to descriptor for the stony mystique that enshrouds many a bottle of wine.

As we examine these mischievous and quirky terms in greater detail, we are compelled to peer deeper into the vocabulary of wine, unburying more obscure and even more evocative descriptors. One might encounter a wine described as having "barnyard" notes - an olfactory trip to the family farm, ushering in visions of haystacks and freckled farmhands, of weathered fences and the raucous crow of a nearby rooster. Smiling, we savor the earthy, somewhat rustic Zinfandel that evokes these images, relishing both the perplexing verbiage and the comforting warmth of its associations.

Or perhaps, in the pursuit of rich, luxurious wines, we find ourselves contemplating the concept of "cigar box" or "tobacconist" - descriptors that swirl with visions of leather armchairs, flickering firelight, and wafts of well-aged tobacco. Even the teetotaler among us cannot help but grin at the notion of a Merlot infused with the poetic scents of cigars, infused with the laughter and camaraderie of gentlemen in their smoking lounges.

In journeying through this labyrinth of descriptor delights, we find our senses sharpened and our laughter bubbling over, like the frothy head on a freshly poured glass of Champagne. For each word we encounter, each phrase that paints an outrageous mental picture, we deepen our appreciation for the playful and perplexing language that cloaks the world of wine.

As we navigate this tantalizing lexicon, let us remember the power that lies in our ability to marvel at the complexities, eccentricities, and the comical incongruities in the realm of wine descriptors. In doing so, we not only broaden our appreciation of the vast tapestry of sensations imbued within each glassful of vino, but we also cultivate the gift of laughter in our every encounter with the arcane and endearing language of wine.

Label Laughs: Embracing Wine Label Misinterpretations and Getting it Right

A great literary mind once said, "Give me wine to wash me clean of the weather-stains of cares." While we can appreciate this earnest entreaty, we must not forget that leaving "weather-stains" of a more literal nature upon our fancy attire is something that we, as wine enthusiasts, endeavor to avoid. But no matter how expertly we refine our swirling technique or valiantly shield our goblets from wine's treacherous splashes, there remains one undeniable truth: it takes an inscrutable eye and discerning mind to decode the miscellany of symbols, words, and typography that graces the label of each bottle.

In this peculiar land of misinterpretation and poetic license, the line between reality and embellishment is delightfully blurred. This hodgepodge of wine label labelsloth leaves ample room for the casual imbiber to be daunted, perplexed or, at times, completely bewildered. It is in this merry chaos that we can find an opportunity to laugh at our own studied attempts at deciphering these cryptic arrays of ink and make a toast to the joys of misinterpretation.

Let us begin with that sly trickster known as typography. From the elegant scrawl of calligraphy that beckons a gentle touch to the loud, jolting meanderings of ornate fonts, each word and letter adorning a wine label conveys a unique character and identity. But oh, how these delicate, artful flourishes can transform a simple request for "Wines of Joy" into an unintended plea for "Wines of Soy" – thus leaving us with the absurd notion of sipping on a saline glass of vinous soy sauce.

Beyond the occasionally befuddling artistic indulgences of the designers, we must brave the quagmire of verbiage found in the arcane realm of translations. As we fumble our way through the tapestry of language, left to contend with foreign tongues and colloquial expressions, we may inadvertently stumble upon amusing (mis)interpretations as delightful as the "mysterious sweet nectar of sweat."

As we revel in these laughable misadventures in translation, we would be remiss not to mention the copious assortment of ambiguous phrases that seem to grace wine labels with an unimaginable frequency. From the enigmatic invitation to be enraptured by the "perfidious charms of Dionysus" to the puzzling advice to "imbibe in moderation or face the wrath of Rabelaisian indulgence," these grandiloquent turns of phrase often lead us DJ down a winding path of furrowed brows and delighted chuckles.

And yet, despite these curious pitfalls and provocations to laughter, we must take solace and even pride in our growing abilities to discern the sordid secrets hidden beneath the layers of ink and artifice. As we venture further into the land of wine label interpretation, let us celebrate our victories – be they small, big or completely ludicrous.

With honed instincts and a burgeoning arsenal of vinous knowledge, we shall pierce the shroud of mystery that enfolds the world of wine labels. In doing so, we embark on a continuous journey of discovery – one filled with baffling typography, improbable translations, and triumphant tales of deciphering the confounding language of wine.

So let us toast to our misinterpretations and misadventures, for each serves as both a lesson and reminder of the importance of maintaining a sense of humor in our pursuit of all things wine. As we continue on this journey, we embrace the possibility of further missteps, confident in the knowledge that these experiences will only serve to enrich our understanding and appreciation of the wines we love.

And if we should once again find ourselves confronted by the poetic puzzle of the wine label, let us remember that the true magic of wine lies within the glass and the moments of laughter and joy that they inspire. In this new-found understanding, may we raise a toast to the eternal power of vinous mirth, emboldened by our misinterpretations and the indomitable spirit of laughter that dwells within each delectable glassful of wine.

Palate Playfulness: Hilariously Mastering Tasting Techniques

How's the taste like?

As we tiptoe, swirl, and savor our way through the dizzying kaleidoscope of the wine world, it is only natural that we eventually encounter the concept of "palate playfulness." A curiously endearing phrase that seems to conjure visions of mirthful taste buds frolicking amidst the vinous delights of each varietal, eager to uncover the secret treasures stashed between the silken folds of flavor and aroma. And yet, as enchanting as these images may be, they belie the intricacy and precision that lie at the heart of mastering the techniques that will elevate our palates to the lofty heights of wine adventuredom.

Indeed, it is within the seemingly whimsical domain of palate playfulness that we find the keys to unlocking the mosaic of the vinous world – and it is with great hilarity and charm that we uncover these secrets. For who among us can resist the lure of a playful showdown between the dancing flavors of citrus and gooseberry, the rambunctious interplay of oak and caramel, or the daring duel between hints of blackberry and cassis?

Let us embark then, hand in hand, upon a rollicking adventure through the blithe world of palatal mischief, where we shall learn to coax secrets from the most demure of Chardonnays, tickle the truth from the most reticent of Shirazes, and cajole whispers of revelation from a stubbornly silent Merlot. And rest assured, dear reader, that along the way we shall indulge in a frolicsome bacchanalia of tastes, textures, and tannins, all the while uncovering the art of hilariously mastering tasting techniques.

As we embark upon this titillating jaunt through the gustatory terrain, it is perhaps prudent to direct our attention first to the most fundamental – and perhaps most deceptively playful – of our tasting techniques: the swirl. While the uninitiated may perceive the swirl as little more than a dalliance designed to invoke an amused smirk or an indulgent sigh, we wily wine lovers know that within the rhythmic undulating of this innocuous gesture lies the secret to unleashing a veritable maelstrom of aromatic and flavor complexities.

And so, we swirl with great (and at times exaggerated) gusto, sending our wines cavorting through the glass in a ritualistic dance that seeks to dislodge even the most recalcitrant and deeply buried of secrets. As delightful and enchanting as this dance may be, we must balance our enthusiasm with a touch of grace and restraint – for, as we have learned, there are few things more chastening to the wine lover's ego than a whirlwind of airborne Cabernet playfully splattering their pristine attire.

Once armed with the power of the swirl, we unfurl our sails and steam forth into the uncharted realms of the tasting process – where an amusing array of textures, tannins, and aftertastes lie in wait, ready to pounce upon our unsuspecting taste buds with the mischievous gleam of impish delight. It is within these storm-tossed seas that we learn to navigate the nuances of mouthfeel, delighting in the plush embrace of a velvety Merlot, gasping at the puckering incursion of a rambunctious young Nebbiolo, and giggling as we attempt to unravel the delicate secrets of a whispery Gewürztraminer.

As we guzzle, sip, and slurp our way through these sensual explorations, we become ever more attuned to the subtleties of flavor and aroma that linger teasingly between each sip – the wisps of raspberry that play hide-and-seek within the folds of a sultry Pinot Noir or the elusive notes of star anise that dart to and fro amidst the heady embrace of an Argentinian Malbec. With each gustatory discovery, we inch closer to the mastery of our playful palates, emboldened by the knowledge that every flirtation with the myriad flavors of the vinous universe unlocks yet another secret within our ever-expanding lexicon of taste.

As we bid farewell to our spirited adventures in palate playfulness, having divined the knowledge and enchanted art that lies within hilariously mastering our tasting techniques, we are left with a warm, lingering sense of buoyancy. For it is within the candy-colored realm of these capricious encounters that we find the heart and soul of the wine world – the light-hearted laughter and flirtatious flavor escapades that inspire and embrace our passion for the delightful complexity and rich tapestry of the wines we love.

And so, resolute and refreshed, we sail onward into uncharted territory, our wines swathed in flavors and memories chased by the playful notes of a bygone symphony. May we toast to the unending pursuit of vinous merriment and the indomitable spirit of laughter that lies within each glass, confident in the knowledge that our mischievous adventures in palate playfulness have only just begun.

Peculiar Palate Preparations: Prepping Your Taste Buds with a Giggle

The vinous landscape stretches before us, a kaleidoscope of flavors, aromas, and textures that beckon our eager taste buds to frolic, gambol, and caper in their most eccentric and peculiar manner. To enter this playground of the senses, we must prepare our palates for the titillating adventure that lies ahead – an adventure filled with laughter, mirth, and perhaps just a hint of whimsy. But beware, for deep within the recesses of our mouths, a comic conspiracy is afoot – our taste buds, those tiny sensory rebels that govern our gustatory predilections, are hard at work devising their next peculiar palate preparation. And in this laugh-laden realm of tongue-tingling caprices, we may find the key to unlocking the mysteries of the world's most fabled potations.

One can hardly imagine a more fitting way to begin the prelude to our peculiar palate preparations than with an exercise that few may regard as anything other than pure gastronomic folly. And yet, to the intrepid devotees of the vintner's art, this exercise is a treasured and core entry to their laughable lexicon – the act of "cleansing" one's palate. Swirling our mouths with a mouthful of water, or better yet, sparkling water, to evict any lingering flavors, we approach this odd ritual with the solemnity of a high priest attending a pagan orgy – tongues wagging, cheeks puffing, and an altogether irreverent explosion of froth and bubbles ensuing. Following this, a long exhalation and perhaps a giggle or snort herald our triumphant entry into the uncharted territories of the palate's preparatory rites.

As we navigate the labyrinthine paths that lead to vinous enlightenment, we may discover that the most peculiar of palate preparations – and perhaps the most comically endearing – lie not only within the depths of our mouths but in our gustatory arsenal of quixotic and comedic technique. Armed with our newfound mastery of palate cleansing, we sally forth into the world of the bizarre and badinage, in search of absurd gustatory discoveries that will leave our taste buds tingling with barely suppressed mirth.

What better way to embark on our peculiar palate preparations than with a foray into the wild and wonderful world of food accoutrements? Here, we tiptoe through the vinous undergrowth in search of the perfect prequel to our libations – a daring dance that pairs the frivolous with the sublime, as we embark on a roller coaster ride of taste sensation and joking jest. Armed with flavor enhancers like lemon, cheese, or even a bite of dark chocolate, we boldly taunt our taste buds' loyalties, ready to draw forth the goofiest of grin.

Once primed and prepped, our taste buds next turn their gustatory gaze toward the hallowed domain of aroma, a place shrouded in mystery, myth, and a good helping of hee-haw. To embark upon this fragrant quest, we tuck our selves into the coziest corners of our most droll dining establishments, surrounded by lavender-scented candles, aged books, and perhaps a plate of freshly prepared Feast of Fancy – a salty slice of prosciutto and a comforting morsel of the finest cheese. Ensconced in our sensory safe haven, we draw forth the revelations of aroma – and inhaled giggles – upon our breath. Wine in hand, we amplify our senses by nosing the wine, like a young bloodhound, sniffing the elusive and amusing scent trace of their next conundrum.

And lest this delightful tapestry of the senses prove too confounding for our tender palates, we call forth the aid of an esoteric compendium of sensory trickery – diversion tactics that serve to confound our taste bud comrades and leave us in a state of delighted hilarity. A burst of mouth puckering sour, a peppery jolt of spice, or the tickling fizz of a soda can send our taste buds scurrying in a comical daze, leaving our gustatory resolve shattered amidst a cacophony of laughter and tongue-tingling delight.

As we forge onward in our peculiar palate preparations, laughing all the way, we embark on a collective journey of discovery and delightful dissipation – indulging in a bacchanalian revelry that celebrates the art of palate puzzle, the play of the senses, and the boundless mirth of the vinous universe. Through our shared hilarity and the wisdom gleaned from these comical gustatory exploits, we continue to hone our skills and deepen our understanding of the wines we cherish – laugh track in tow. From mastering a snicker to a full-throated cackle, we approach each new adventure in palate preparation with humor, wit, and a twinkle in our eyes, confident in the knowledge that hilarity truly is the best wine of life.

The Nose Knows: Sniffing for Sarcasm and Subtle Bouquets

Within the whimsical realm of wine appreciation, we venture forth into a terrain often shrouded in myth and misconception – for it is within the swirling mists of the vine's most fragrant domain that we find our most potent ally: our powerful sense of smell. Aptly described as the "nose" of wine, the truest and most nuanced of a wine's aromatic expressions can be discovered only through the artful application of our olfactory faculties and the keen diversification of our nasal sensitivities. In doing so, we will uncover a delightful world of subtle bouquets, pungent perfumes, and unexpected sensory delights that will surely leave us with tippling tales, copious hysterics, and a renewed appreciation for the fine art of laughter.

As we embark upon the giddy journey of honing our nostril prowess, we would do well to remember the sage words of one of history's great oenophiles: "The first duty of wine is to be aromatic, and the second is to have a sense of humor." And indeed, it is within these guiding principles that we shall endeavor to explore the surreptitious realm of olfactory delights hidden within each glass.

Our first order of business in becoming masters of the wine-sniffing game lies in acquainting ourselves with the basic rules of engagement. With the glass at an angle, swirling the wine within, we lower our noses to the rim and partake in a series of rapid inhalations, each sip of air more revealing than the last. Underlying notes of crushed rose petals, tobacco, ripe plums, and perhaps just a hint of playful sarcasm begin to unfurl from their hiding places, imbuing the glass with an effusion of fragrance, character, and wit.

But, dear reader, our humorous aromatic adventure is far from over. For within the swirling dance of scent molecules released by our dutifully swirling wine, we may find more resonant tales that beg to be uncovered. Did a sprightly double entendre just dash across the glass? Was that a whiff of well-placed irony that caused our nose to wrinkle just a touch? Indeed, it is within the constant interplay of aroma and wit that we find the most engaging and beguiling aspect of wine appreciation.

Of course, these scented witticisms do not reveal themselves easily. They require keen observation, a fearless nose, and perhaps a dash of silly intuition to coax them from their hiding places. To achieve this, we must practice our sniffing and breathing techniques with dedicated fervor and comical ambition, filling our nostrils with the potent vocabulary of the vine until we can discern, with exquisite accuracy, the secret notes of honey, spice, and the most evanescent of punchlines that may dwell within the heart of even the most reticent of vintages.

Once the foundations of this razor-sharp nasal dexterity have been laid, we find ourselves on the precipice of scented nirvana – a realm where we can divine the mysteries of terroir, varietal, age and the sass of our favorite wine with the tilt of our noses and a sly wink aimed at the sommelier.

It is not long before we find our gustatory adventures infused with these engaging threads of ribald banter, each sniff unlocking a new trove of pun-laden epigrams and tongue-in-cheek observations that some may argue are essential to the true appreciation of the secrets of the vine. It is in such moments, with our olfactory faculties scrubbed clean and our senses precariously perched at the pinnacle of subtle sarcasm detection, that our journey into wine enlightenment takes another bold leap into the realms of whimsy and wonder.

As we journey through the realms of wine and laughter, we may summon the pithy aphorisms and quicksilver observations from our comically tinged libations. We find in our glasses a treasure trove of wit and wisdom, from the cheeky joke that graces our Chardonnay to the tongue-tingling limerick dancing atop our Port, all conspiring to engage our senses and wit in a veritable symphony of comedic revelry.

As we raise our glasses in celebration of these enigmatic aromatic encounters, we proudly proclaim nez du vin – a toast to the wit and wisdom gleaned from the wine's most mysterious and playful realm. And as we partake of its many pleasures, we remain, forever, the tenacious seekers of scent and comedy, striding forth into the vinous landscape with nostrils flaring and our hearts filled with laughter. For ultimately, in wine and life, it is through the power of our noses and the loves of our laughter that we find the most profound and resonant moments of connection – a duality that, when embraced with both humor and passion, can elevate even the humblest of libations to heights heretofore unimagined.

Silly Sipping Strategies: Maneuvering Wine in Your Mouth like a Pro (and Comedian)

The road to becoming a sommelier-extraordinaire – and a cork-er of a comedian – is fraught with tempting detours, beguiling distractions, and the odd pratfall that leaves one's ego as bruised as the forgotten grapes that never make it into the wine press. Yet, fear not, for in the realm of libations and laughter, these hiccups are but the meandering journey that will lead us to the heart of the matter: mastering the art of silly sipping strategies.

Indeed, such silly sipping strategies are the rainbow-striped umbrellas that adorn our proverbial wine glasses as we traverse the delightful and occasionally foolish landscape of the absurd. These methods – like the colorful plumage of a majestic bird of paradise – serve to signal to our fellow sippers that we are, indeed, worthy, vigilant, and whimsical participants in the game of wine appreciation.

We must first cast our gaze upon the most fundamental of such silly sipping methods: the art of aerating wine within our mouths. While lesser mortals might simply slug their libations with reckless abandon, we intrepid souls embrace the challenge of becoming human decanters – our cheeks billowing like sails upon the high seas as we welcome the incoming tide of fermented nectar. With gusto and unwavering commitment, we slosh, swoosh, and even gargle our way through claret, Chardonnay, and all that lies between, all the while feeling the embrace of a most peculiar tongue tango with every twist and turn of our libational ministrations.

Next, we turn our attention to the subtle and seductive art of the wine-in-cheek maneuver – a technique that is, perhaps, best remembered as the Picasso of our palette's playful pleasures. Like the skilled artist who embraces the curious commingling of abstraction and puckish wit, we find ourselves navigating the curious interplay of bitterness, sweetness, and the delectable hint of humor that can be found in the most surprising of liquid couplings.

Here, our penchant for playfulness is rewarded with the exquisite discovery that even the humblest of swills can be elevated to a symphony of sensation and whimsy with but the merest flick of one's tongue and a mischievous gleam in one's eye.

As we hone these foundational skills of our silly sipping stratagem, we begin to discover that the sky is, indeed, the limit when it comes to exploring the vast possibilities that lie within our mouths and our minds. Much like the dexterous fingers of a concert pianist, we learn to coax a cacophony of flavors, textures, and amusing asides from the depths of our fickle fluids, using our tongue to create symphonies that would leave Mozart green with envy.

Armed with our newfound mastery of the human decanting arts, we embark on our next foray into the world of silly sipping methods: the inverted sip. This unguarded and perhaps bizarre approach to tasting wine is indeed an act of devil-may-care courage – tilting our heads back ever so delicately, allowing a modest sip of wine to dangle precariously on the precipice of our chins before inviting it to make a hasty retreat down our throats in an unexpected direction. The result? An eruption of giggles and chortles that borders on the scandalous and shakes the very foundations of enological propriety.

As we venture further down the rabbit hole of our peculiar vinous Wonderland, we encounter a wealth of techniques and tactics that serve to keep our taste buds, and our funny bones, ever agile and on their toes. The noble slurp, the daring swill, and even the oft-maligned reverse gargle, all conspire to create a rollicking, sprite-like dance within our mouths that might leave our fellow wine enthusiasts in paroxysms of laughter – or tutting disapprovingly, depending on the level of their own oenological commitment.

Yet, it is through these comic escapades and gustatory escapisms that we ultimately lay claim to the most coveted prize of all: the hallowed state of silly sipper supreme, a title bestowed upon only the most audacious and daring of wine adventurers. Formidable but never fussy; charismatic but never cloying, we become the living embodiment of terpsichorean terroir, our tongues pirouetting giddily through lush vineyards and jesting jest along the way.

As we continue our journey through the boundless fields of fermented frivolity and the titillating territory between grape and glass, we find ourselves not only fortified by the liquid treasures cradled within our cups, but by the indomitable spirit of our intrepid, laughing hearts. For in the most unexpected of moments, amongst the swirling aromas and the clinking of glasses, we may discover the true essence of what it means to embrace the world of wine with a smile, a wink, and a bit of knowing cackle – forging forth into a future where vinous virtuosity and unbridled hilarity walk hand-in-hand, for all our sipping days to come.

Playing with Texture: A Comical Guide to Describing Wine's Feel on Your Tongue

As we saunter hand in hand with whimsy and wonder through the glorious gardens of all things enological, we inevitably stumble upon a particularly peculiar patch of vines - for it is here, in the verdant embrace of the vine's most tactile domain, that we fathom the unfathomable, grasp the ungraspable, and touch the intangible, within the swirling maelstrom of our mouths: the realm of texture.

To be sure, no wine adventure can ever truly be considered complete without some forays into the labyrinthine, tactile world of vinous viscosity, where we balance precariously on the edge of audacity. For it is only when we careen headlong into the abyss of gustatory gymnastics that we can ever hope to unravel the supple mysteries of the wine's touch, taste, and titillating tactile sensation upon our tongues.

In such pursuits, we must arm ourselves with an array of silver-tongued strategies, each more daring and dexterous than the last. With the agility of a tightrope walker, the precision of a surgeon, and the cunning of a fox, we endeavor to sweep our probing instruments across the surface of myriad wines, plumbing the depths of their velvety secrets with the deft proficiency of a seasoned scuba diver.

To begin with, the fundamental tool of our trade must be the simple-yet-efficacious technique known as the "wine whisperer." Here, we allow ourselves to be guided by our tongue's ability to coax and cajole even the most recalcitrant of wines into a medley of molten disclosure. With a gentle caress, a tender touch, and a flirtatious flick, our devoted taste buds summon forth the kaleidoscope of sensations that dance beneath the surface; as slippery as a fish, as supple as a kitten, and as silky as a well-worn stocking.

Once we have familiarized ourselves with the foundational art of the wine whisperer, we can proceed to dabble in the more esoteric realms of textured tomfoolery. Entering the hallowed halls of gustatory prestidigitation, we might find ourselves wielding such tactics as the "terroir tango," the "varietal vault," and even the "tannic tickle" with the lithe grace and precision of a prize-winning figure skater.

In conducting these daring textual high jinks, we engage in a veritable pas de deux with our libational partner, each step, pirouette, and spin a testimony to our unwavering dedication to the pursuit of texture and the preservation of its truest, most effervescent expressions.

But beware, dear reader, for the tactile terrain that we embark upon is littered with perilous pitfalls, like berries strewn upon the wine-splattered path of our vinous escapades. Overzealous execution of the "terroir tango" might leave us in a tangled heap, our tongues undoing the subtle latticework of taste that had been so artfully interwoven by the once-eager grapes.

Fumbling the "varietal vault" will likely result in a near-farcical crash landing, our mendacious mouths reduced to rueful grimaces as we attempt to extricate ourselves and our pride from the velvety embrace of defeat.

And lastly, a misapplied "tannic tickle" may well end in ribald raillery and disapproving clucks from our fellow sippers, as we find ourselves grappling with the inescapable question: "Have we gone too far in our quest for tactile triumph?"

Yet even in the face of such grievous gaffes, we must persevere in our pursuit of textured mastery; for it is only through failure, like the discarded lees of yesterday's ferment, that we can rise, phoenix-like, to new heights of tenacity and understanding.

As we march forth into the textured wilds with our heads high and our tongues unfurled, let us take solace that it is through our diligent exploration, our unwavering pursuit of gustatory ecstasy, and our willingness to dance with the fickle dame of texture that we can ever hope to savor the unfettered essence of wine and laughter, the holy grail of sass and silk.

Through tactile exploration, pitched playfully between amusement and insight, we find new dimensions of connection with our beloved nectar. As we raise our glasses and salute the myriad textures that dazzle our mouths and fire our imaginations, we shall continue to drink deeply from the heady brew of laughter and wit in equal measure. Now, armed with an innovative repertoire of linguistic acrobatics, we may disseminate these newfound amusements, sharing our revelations over animated banter and flowing glasses. May the peal of our laughter be ever more transcendent when underscored by the exquisite splendor of wine's nuanced caress upon our eager palates.

Laughing at Legginess: What Wine Legs Really Tell Us (Hint: It's Not about the Wine's Dancing Skills)

As we continue our pilgrimage through the vast vineyards of hilarity and tongue-in-cheek oenological appreciation, we cannot help but pause, mid-gallop, and cast a curious eye upon a peculiar phenomenon that has long beguiled and bemused even the most seasoned of sippers amongst us: the enigmatic, somewhat mesmerizing presence of wine legs.

Yes, those spindly tendrils of vinous brilliance that slide ever-so-sensuously down the inside of our glorious glassware, as if beckoning us to delve deeper into the liquid treasures contained within. In fact, one might be forgiven for assuming, at first glance, that these beguiling streaks are of paramount importance in the evaluation of a wine's worth – a webbed network of clues that might reveal mysteries unknown to even the most astute of palates.

But do not be deceived, dear fellow wine aficionados, for these legs – as tantalizing and tempting as they may appear – are, in fact, little more than a fickle distraction from the true treasures nestled within our olfactory and gustatory playground. Indeed, the significance of the wine leg exhibition is about as consequential as the flamenco dance skills of a flamingo – attention-grabbing and splendid, perhaps, but ultimately bearing no weight on the liquid's innate merits.

Allow us to explain: wine legs, in their simplest form, are a visible manifestation of the interaction between the potent powers of alcohol and the considerably more demure forces of surface tension, capillary action, and evaporation. In essence, this delicate interplay of forces serves to create minuscule rivers within the glass, as the higher alcohol content seeks to rise above its watery peers and join the lofty company of the ether. In doing so, the wine's unsung heroes – water molecules, with their unbreakable cohesion and stoic endurance – struggle valiantly to hold the line and maintain their grip on the swirling mass below, creating a thrilling cascade of dribbles and drizzles with each deft rotation of the wrist.

Yet, while this visual display might be a source of much interest and fascination – conjuring images, perhaps, of a microscopic Cirque du Soleil, with trapeze artists, tightrope walkers, and swirling dervishes hidden within the very fabric of our wine – it is crucial to remember that such acrobatic feats have little bearing on the tastiness and quality of the wine at hand. While some may argue that the legs are indicative of a wine's alcohol content, it is important to recognize that a sound judgment of a libation's inherent value cannot be gleaned from these liquid cartwheels.

Rather, we must strive to see beyond the siren-like allure of these shimmering streams, and cast our sensory nets ever deeper into the vast oceans of taste, aroma, and laugh-inducing merriment that are the true raison d'être of our delightful encounters with Bacchus' bounty.

In addition, it is worth noting that, just as our beloved wine legs have little bearing on a wine's worthiness of our esteem, so too do such spider-legged marvels often elicit a chuckle from our funny bones. For in the midst of vinous contemplation and scholarly discernment, there is ample room for the occasional sideways glance and sly grin as we gaze upon the countless tales and adventures that have been spun – quite literally – by the riotous exploits of our precious beverage's limbs.

So the next time you are presented with a glass of vino, resplendent with arachnid-esque limbs that skitter and scurry, fret not about the potential veracity of these misleading appendages. Instead, raise a toast to the inherent silliness of life, the absurdity of existence, and the unending delight that can be found in both the rib-tickling antics of wine, and the kaleidoscopic array of experiences that await within every glorious sip. For though the fleeting footprint of the wine leg may hold little sway over the mysterious melodies that dance through the timbre of our tastebuds, it is but one more reason to revel in the grand symphony of laughter and life that are interwoven into the very fabric of that most noble and sudoriferous endeavor: the finding and enjoying of the divine nectar of the gods, while ever ready to indulge the Urge of the Urgent Jests that will echo throughout the halls of both history and temptation.

The Fun Finish: Unraveling the Aftertaste with Wit and Wisdom

Ah, the aftertaste - that ephemeral, ever-elusive echo of a wine's true essence that lingers like a haunting melody, long after the curtain has fallen on its sumptuous opening act. Indeed, it is within the fleeting whispers of this wraithlike reverberation that we find the most colorful threads of flavor; a cacophonous tapestry of tart and tangy, profound and playful, swooning, and dizzyingly delightful. And it is these very characteristics that serve as the lifeblood of our vinous pursuits, spanning the gamut from humorous daydreams to sage wisdom.

But how are we to unravel the gossamer strands of countertaste, to fully fathom the richness of character locked within these coy and capricious couriers of the tongue? Our quest lies within, as we delve into the intricate world of finish and aftertaste with wit, wisdom, and a penchant for the absurd.

Let us begin our foray into this veritable rabbit hole of the senses by considering the all-important factor that distinguishes a wine's aftertaste from its more immediate neighbors - duration. For, much like the theatrical encore of a skilled thespian, it is the length of a wine's finish that can reveal much about its character, be it a thoughtful soliloquy or a boisterous slapstick routine.

But there is more to the art of aftertaste appreciation than simply timing. We must also consider the complexity and intensity of flavors that color our experience, transforming even the briefest of encounters into a symphony of sensory delight. A crescendo of effervescent tartness, a quixotic rhapsody of floral refrain, a riotous overture of nutty undertones – each playing a unique role within the tempestuous dance of taste that inhabits the sacred space between sips.

And, as we waltz through the swirling maelstrom of flavor that ensconces our tongues and teases our minds, it is of paramount importance that we approach the finicky funambulist of finish with a keen wit and a judicious sense of humor. For, in embracing the delightful and ludicrous, we can enter into a richer dimension of appreciation for our beloved vino's coy game of hide-and-seek.

With a knowing wink and a playful grin, we may marvel at the audacity of a red so bold that it lingers like the ink-stained fingers of a ne'er-do-well in a mirthful midnight scrawl upon the palate. Or, perhaps, lose ourselves in the giddy symphony of a white that pirouettes through our senses, a veritable wine waltz of froth and effervescence that echoes of sunshine and seaspray.

Yet, it is not enough to simply flirt with the shadows of the gustatory demi-monde – we must also engage our sense of wisdom, for it is within the hallowed halls of thoughtful reflection that we can uncover the true nature of any given finish. As the esteemed philosopher, Heraclitus, once opined, "wine makes the wisest man do foolish things" - and yet, as oenophiles, are these very follies not the splendiferous jewels that illuminate our paths of discovery?

Such are the questions that tantalize our tastebuds and wrap our tongues in vanished veils of gusto. And it is in these hallways of insightful reverie, walking hand-in-hand with wit and wisdom, that we may extend our exploration of the aftertaste beyond the boundaries of the glass, and thereby challenge our minds and hearts in a quest for an ever greater appreciation of the beloved libations that giddily dance upon our tongues.

Though we navigate the nebulous wonders of wine's aftertaste, a shared chuckle and raised glass later, it is in the artful embrace of both the subtle and the sublime that we find the courage to delve deeper, venturing forth with newfound vigor and anticipation – eager to explore the boundless bounty of our beloved grape's final gift: The Fun Finish, to be shared, savored, and celebrated with a fusion of unwieldy humor and profound wisdom. And as we depart from this fleeting foray into wine world reverie, let our laughter ring through the tapestried halls of memory - a testament to the wild-eyed whispers of countless kisses from Bacchus' bountiful obsession.

The Tasting Takeaway: Quirky Tips and Mind-blowing Memorable Moments to Share with Friends

As our exhilarating journey through the winding labyrinth of vinous delights begins to draw to a close, we find ourselves faced with the daunting task of distilling the essence of our numerous into a potent elixir that we might carry with us into the world beyond the rim of our glass. It is here, in the crucible of memory and experience, that we must forge our tasting takeaways, using the whimsical fires of our humor as fuel and the steadfast hammer of our insight as guidance. For it is only by combining these two vital ingredients – the laughter that keeps our spirits buoyant and the wisdom that reminds us of what truly matters – that we can hope to create a concoction worthy of the Vin de Vie's remarkable legacy.

One of the most essential lessons we have gleaned over our time exploring the hallowed halls of hilarity and hedonism is that, at its core, wine is a truly multifaceted creature – a chameleon that teaches us as much about ourselves as it does about itself. Each swirl, sniff, and sip has brought with it a new revelation, exposing hidden dimensions of character that have simultaneously astonished, delighted, and transported us to far off realms of giddy fancy.

But how might we package these innumerable pearls of wisdom into a single, cogent message that will withstand the test of time and ensure their lasting impact upon our senses?

The key, dear friends, lies in recognizing that wine, like life itself, is a wonderfully complex tapestry of interconnected threads, weaving together myriad experiences, emotions, and flavors into a vibrant and harmonious whole. And, just as our own lives are inexorably shaped by the myriad interactions and encounters that befall us in this vast cosmic dance, so, too, are our glorious glasses of vino infinitely enriched by the seemingly endless streams of wit and wisdom distilled within their warm, liquid embrace.

In this way, we must not only remember to savor the fleeting gifts of our cherished libations – that delicious interplay of taste, texture, and aroma that has nourished our very souls for the duration of our pilgrimage – but also, crucially, to carry those magical moments forward with us into the world beyond the glass. For it is only by sharing these joyous experiences with our fellow travelers in this grand journey, that we can hope to keep the indomitable spirit of wine alive and burning brightly in our hearts.

And so, with our tasting takeaway in hand, let us tarry no longer in the solitary sanctum of the oenophile – the time has come to burst forth from the warm cocoon of flame-kissed vine and fragrant bouquet, and join the merry throng beyond! It is there, amidst the laughter and embraces of our nearest and dearest, that we shall find the true measure of wine's gift, and witness the remarkable alchemy of joy and unity that is wrought when we share the fruits of our gustatory adventures with those we hold most dear.

As we venture forth into the bustling cacophony of life, let us always remember the many lessons our precious grape libations have taught us, for it is within the rich tapestry of sips and stories that we find much-needed oases of joy and laughter. Whether we are regaling our loved ones with tales of runaway reds, gallant whites, or swooning rosés, we can be confident that our words will fall on attentive ears and kindred spirits, eager to join us in the glorious reverie that is the world of wine.

And so, we charge you, noble oenophiles, to heed the clarion call of this, our final decree, and take to the fields, hills, and dales of friendship and festivity – bearing in your hands the sacred keys to Bacchus' treasure trove, and in your hearts the indomitable spirit of laughter and light. Let these potent tools serve as your lodestar, guiding you to new heights of joy and camaraderie, and reminding you always of the wondrous power of a well-told tale spun beneath the shimmering tapestry of our shared love of wine and laughter.

As you embark on this sacred mission, gaze up at the horizon with the knowledge that each quirk, tip, and memorable moment shared becomes a golden thread weaving our collective tales, and as we stand united in this kaleidoscopic odyssey, we are bound by the inescapable truth that it is the courageous, the hilarious, and the ever-lasting enchantment of the vinous kingdom that unites us all in giddy delight and, ultimately, transcendent understanding.

Grapey Gab: Amusing Wine Lingo for Wine Newbies

Lost in the woods…?

It was the great sage of vinology, William Shakespeare, who once penned the immortal phrase: "A grape by any other name would taste as sweet." Or something to that effect. For as our intrepid journey through the rolling vineyards of wine appreciation has taught us, wine – like the language used to describe it – is a fluid and ever-shifting creature, an amorphous wisp of aroma and taste that has beguiled scholars, poets, and everyday tipplers alike for millennia.

And so, we arrive at the heart of the matter – an exploration into the dizzying realms of wine lingo, where poetic flights of fancy collide with technical jargon in a merry, swirling dance of truth and embellishment. Here, we shall endeavor to peel back the layers of grapey gab, exposing the shining nuggets of wit and wisdom buried 'neath the shadowy depths of cant and argot, and emerging triumphantly into the sunlit meadows of clarity and comprehension.

Before we can truly ponder the intricacies of lofty descriptors, however, we must first acquaint ourselves with the basic literary building blocks that form the foundation of wine appreciation. Let us begin with the lowly grape, that humble and yet altogether noble fruit which is the progenitor of every vintage and varietal since time immemorial. In addition to providing the basic juice that is the very lifeblood of vino, grapes also lend their names to the numerous colorful terms that pepper the discourse of oenophiles everywhere.

To wit, consider the bright-hued lexicon of "jammy," which conjures visions of delectable, sun-kissed fruits spread generously upon the welcoming canvas of the palate. Or, cast your mind's eye upon "foxy," evoking the crafty and cunning of the woodland denizen, as we delve into the more enigmatic side of winemaking in which wild and rustic tastes trill a tantalizing, elusive melody that dances upon our tongues. Not to be outdone, we have "bacchinalian" - a term synonymous with Dionysian revelry and unabashed indulgence that is often used without a hint of irony to describe wines of an opulent, powerful character.

As we have seen, the language of wine can be equally rich and diverse as the vino itself. But our lexical odyssey does not stop there, for we must also contend with the more arcane and esoteric terms that inhabit the hallowed halls of wine jargon. For example, take the cryptic, and at times bewildering, term "terroir" - a word borrowed from French that refers to the specific environmental factors affecting a wine's character, such as soil and climate.

While terroir may elicit befuddled head-scratching from even the most seasoned of oenophiles, it is a concept of vital importance, as it encapsulates the ever-elusive and oft-debated influence of geography, geology, and meteorology upon the taste, texture, and finish of the wines that we so cherish. In a world where wine appreciation is increasingly dominated by global sameness, terroir represents a steadfast bulwark against the encroaching tide of homogenization – a veritable crucible of character, within which the distinctive essence of each unique vintage can forge its own identity and style.

But let us not be too hasty in our dismissal of technical jargon, for such terms also offer a window into the world of science and craftsmanship that underpins the art of winemaking. Consider, for instance, the seemingly innocuous phrase "malolactic fermentation." At first glance, it may appear as nothing more than a laboratory buzzword devoid of humor or charm, yet this humble process forms the backbone of countless velvety, full-bodied reds and even some headstrong, stubborn whites that grace our tables and warm our hearts.

In this way, by turning our gaze to the underbelly of wine lingo – to the nuts and bolts, the nuts and grapes, if you will – we can gain newfound appreciation for the myriad factors that conspire to transmute humble vine juice into the nectar of the gods.

As we now pause to reflect upon the vast tapestry of wine language that we have sampled, we must not forget that the ultimate purpose of this lexicon is not to bewilder or intimidate, but rather to unite us in our shared love for the grape. For wine, like life itself, is a journey of discovery – an endless odyssey of learning that traverses the very depths of our olfactory senses, stirring our souls and nourishing our minds with a delightful interplay of aromas, tastes, and textures.

The Language of Lushes: An Introduction to Wine Lingo

The setting sun casts a rich, golden glow over the vineyards as we gather at the table, each bearing our chosen libation to share with our brethren in this merry, Dionysian repast. Yet before we can uncork our purple elixirs and savor their intoxicating bouquet, we must first engage in a ritual as old as winemaking itself – the age-old dance of wine lingo.

For as the great Robert Mondavi once observed, "Wine is the most civilized conversation opener... and best enjoyed when words are a part of the evening's enjoyment." And so, as we join our friends and fellow oenophiles in this gustatory celebration, we must endeavor to become fluent in the arcane and whimsical argot of our cherished libations – to master the tongue of Bacchus himself and weave our own wondrous tapestry of wine-soaked revelry.

But where, pray tell, does one begin on this epic journey into the world of wine lingo? Let us start, as all brave explorers must, at the very beginning: the humble grape – that wondrous orb of alchemy that provides the very substrate upon which this intoxicating symphony is built.

As inhabitants of a thoroughly globalized world and with a wealth of vinous possibilities at our fingertips, we are spoiled for choice when it comes to selecting our preferred poison. And with such a dizzying array of varietals and vintages on offer, it is only natural that we turn to language to help us navigate this sea of vinous plenty. Yet it is not enough to simply be able to rattle off a list of grape varieties or regions like a sommelier worth his creed; one must delve deeper into the expressive lexicon of wine language and uncover the hidden trove of evocative imagery that awaits within.

For example, consider the term "legs." At first blush, one might question the relevance of such a word in an oenophilic context, reasoning that it should be reserved for discussions of bipeds and furniture. Yet, in a wine lover's parlance, legs possess a far more nuanced meaning – they are the trails left on the glass as you tilt it, tracing your wine's cartography through its alcoholic and textural essence. While this term may seem comical and absurdly detached from the subject at hand, it serves as an intriguing invitation to approach wine tasting with a sense of humor and whimsy, transforming it from a stuffy pastime into a more lighthearted adventure.

And what of the more esoteric terminology that adorns our wine labels and tasting notes? Take, for instance, "mouthfeel" – that ineffable quality that describes how a wine coats our palates, enveloping our senses in its velvety grasp. This seemingly innocuous descriptor may initially provoke a chuckle at its bawdy implications, yet upon deeper reflection, it provides a perfect vehicle for communicating the tactile experience of sipping wine – an experience that is all too often overshadowed by our obsession with taste and aroma.

As we delve further into the rabbit hole of wine language, we begin to uncover a veritable treasure trove of luscious imagery, evoking landscapes of lush vineyards, sun-dappled orchards, and pillowy banks of meringue. Phrases such as "racy acidity," "flinty minerality," and "autolytic toast" might initially seem more suited to a surrealist painting than a wine review, yet each of these expressions serves as a vital portal into the ever-shifting realm of wine appreciation, transporting our senses to far-off worlds and allowing us to taste, if only for a fleeting moment, the transcendent nectar of the gods.

As we now pause to catch our breath and take stock of our newfound knowledge, it is our solemn duty to bear in mind that the ultimate purpose of wine language is not to bewilder and befuddle but rather to unite us in our shared love for the grape. For, as the great poet Paul Valéry once declared, “wine is a civilizing agent… it makes us aware of subtleties, it increases our capacity for pleasure; it teaches us the effects of volatile substances on the nervous system.”

In this spirit, let us raise our glasses and toast to the gift of language – that glorious vehicle of human expression that allows us to bridge the vast and ever-changing landscape of wine and laughter, unlocking the secrets of this magical libation and sharing our discoveries with friends and fellow travelers in this grand symphony of life. For as the flames of friendship burn ever brighter, we are reminded of the words of the inimitable Muriel Barbery: "wine is alive, and if its complex flavors do not trouble your mind and delight your heart, then it is not wine."

Uncorking the Connoisseur: Decoding Wine Jargon for Dummies

If humanity and its multifarious interpretations of reality can be likened to a kaleidoscope, then our journey through the mystifying realm of wine jargon is like being trapped within a dizzying, refracted dance of terminology and metaphor. We hurry past swirling mirages of vinous description, sidestepping the alluring diversion of grandiose appellations that threaten to swallow us whole in their whirlwind of verbosity. But fear not, intrepid traveler, for our linguistic odyssey is one of unraveling complexity, of stripping back the layers of grandiloquent excess and arriving, windswept and grinning, at the crystal core of comprehension.

In seeking to uncork the connoisseur – that elusive, erudite creature that dwells deep within each of us – we must first wrest ourselves from the tangled tendrils of jargon. Like Theseus in the labyrinth, we carry only our sharpened wits and an unwavering commitment to clarity, as we gently peel away the strands of vinous hyperbole that ensnare our fellow journeyers. The Minotaur of wine-speak is not slain in one swift stroke; rather, we must gradually dismantle its fearsome grip on our collective psyche, revealing the fragile skeleton of language upon which it is built.

Take, for instance, the infamous term "bouquet." As though plucked from the luxuriant boughs of an enchanted forest, this poetic descriptor paves the way for a cacophony of similes and allegory, transforming the act of wine appreciation into a stroll through a fragrant garden of literary delights. On the surface, bouquet might seem little more than a pretentious synonym for aroma or scent, yet the discerning oenophile will recognize in its complex etymology a rich tapestry of historical, cultural and botanical references that underpin its true meaning. Deftly wielded, bouquet is a potent weapon in the connoisseur's arsenal, capable of conjuring evocative images of far-off lands and lost epochs from the delicate waft of a carefully-swirled glass.

Moving on, let us now turn our focus to structure, an oft-misunderstood term that straddles the worlds of physical science and phenomenological subjectivity. Drawing inspiration from the architectural lexicon, structure describes the interplay of elements such as acidity, tannins, and alcohol within a given wine, creating a harmonious whole that transcends the sum of its parts. As any seasoned oenophiliac will attest, a wine lacking structure is a crumbling edifice of disappointment – a feeble construct that cannot sustain the weight of its lofty ambitions. Fortified with the knowledge of structure, we are better equipped to assess a wine's overall balance and quality, with a nod to both empirical rigidity and sensory perception.

No exploration of wine jargon would be complete without a brief sojourn into the seductive world of finish – a term that brings to mind the final surging crescendo of a symphony, as the baton descends and the curtain falls. To the uninitiated, finish might simply denote the aftertaste that lingers on one's tongue post-swallow, but the true connoisseur understands it to encompass far more. A wine's finish carries within it echoes of terroir, blending artistry, and aging potential, contributing to the greater gestalt of the tasting experience. When we extol the virtues of a long, smooth finish, we are connecting with a fundamental aspect of wine appreciation – the transportive power of a vinous dénouement that lingers in the memory like a whispered refrain.

It would be remiss of us not to pay homage to one of the most divisive, enthralling, and delightfully esoteric words in the wine-speak canon – minerality. Conjuring images of rocky outcrops, stony beaches, and windswept mountaintops, this term evoking terroir's elemental side has invited both ardent devotion and snide derision in equal measure. While some insist on its inclusion in any serious oenophilic lexicon, others deride it as a vague, unscientific portmanteau of wine mysticism. Yet, as we have seen throughout our adventures in decoding wine jargon, it is within these gray areas – these shifting sands of linguistic uncertainty – that the true spirit of wine appreciation is to be found.

Armed now with a veritable arsenal of wine-speak weaponry, our adventure through the labyrinthine tunnels of jargon and exaggeration draws to a close. But fear not, for we have not merely navigated past the fearsome Minotaur; we have tamed and harnessed its power, crafting an incisive and formidable vocabulary that can slice through the densest thicket of jargon and spin dazzling linguistic skeins in equal measure. As we advance with renewed confidence and clarity into the world beyond the labyrinth, we carry with us our hard-won knowledge, poised to navigate the intricate landscape of wine appreciation and savor the intoxicating mélange of descriptors that lie in wait.

Whining in Wine: The Funniest Wine Terminology You Never Knew Existed

As we have wandered through the hallowed halls of wine wisdom, we have navigated the labyrinthine troves of vocabularies and wandered through the twisted vines of wine jargon. In our quest for vinous fluency, we have mastered the art of swirling and sniffing, deciphered the arcane texts of wine labels, and honed our senses to distinguish the most delicate of bouquets. But now, dear reader, we stand upon the precipice of a wonderous revelation, a discovery that will forever change the way we think, feel, and communicate about our beloved nectar of the gods.

For in shedding light on the overlooked and underappreciated corners of wine terminology, we have uncovered that which eludes even the most seasoned of oenophiles: the realm of the hilarious, the absurd, and the utterly delightful. Prepare to embark on the whimsical journey that lies ahead, as we delve into the world of the funniest wine terminology you never knew existed.

To begin, we must first acquaint ourselves with the term "cork-tease," a cheeky nod to those who, in the amorous dance of wine appreciation, tantalize our senses with the promise of an exquisite vintage yet cruelly withhold the pleasure of partaking. As we chuckle at this playful pun, we can almost see the scene unfold before us: the ambrosial elixir proffered, a glinting corkscrew at the ready, only to be snatched away at the last moment, leaving us longing for the sweet kiss of fermented fruit denied.

Our journey through the recesses of vinous humor soon brings us face-to-face with the "wine gnome," an enigmatic figure who lurks in the shadows of wine-tasting lore, snickering at our feeble attempts to grasp its true nature. As we sip and savor, we may sometimes catch a glimpse of this elusive creature, lurking behind a glass of murky sediment-laden vintage or popping up unexpectedly in the midst of a heated debate over the merits of stemware. Yet, as quickly as we spy the wine gnome, it vanishes, leaving us to ponder the real meaning of our shared wine-imbibing experience.

We continue our light-hearted sojourn by raising a glass to a most unusual phenomenon, the "cat's pee" descriptor. While we may balk at the thought of feline effluvia finding its way into our wine, we cannot help but titter at this odd and audacious idiom. Amidst laughter and raised eyebrows, it emerges that this peculiar phrase is used to describe the sharp, pungent aroma of some Sauvignon Blanc wines, setting the stage for intriguing wine conversations that will no doubt give us pause – or should we say, "paws"?

As we meander through the maze of riotous wine jargon, we stumble upon a term that has our heads spinning faster than a glass of Shiraz at a tasting – "Brixplanation." At first, we may be struck by confusion, wondering whether we have unwittingly intruded on a discussion about winemaking decibels. Yet, with mirthful illumination, we discover that this term cleverly satirizes the practice of elevating Brix – a measure of a grape's sugar content – as the ultimate arbiter of a wine's quality, thereby poking fun at those who approach wine appreciation with undue seriousness and dogmatism.

No comedic lexicon of wine terms could ever be deemed complete without a nod to the whimsical and bizarre world of "fruit bombs." Seemingly plucked straight from a comic-strip universe, this endearing descriptor conjures images of explosive cherries, detonating peaches, and cataclysmic bursts of berries. Though we may ponder the implications of such a volatile vinous vocabulary, we soon realize that fruit bombs simply signify wines that are overflowing with ripe fruit flavors, eliciting smirks and grins as we share our newfound knowledge with fellow wine enthusiasts.

As we round the final bend of our hilarious, tongue-in-cheek tour of wine terminology, we bid farewell to preconceived notions, stodginess, and dull relatability. Wine, after all, is not simply a beverage of pomp and privilege; it is a libation that unites us in an eternal dance of laughter, camaraderie, and exploration. In our quest to decode the mysteries of vinous language, let us remember to embrace the world of witticisms, puns, and far-fetched metaphors, and may our own wine speak ever be imbued with the sparkle of mischief and mirth.

For as we emerge from this spirited odyssey of whimsical wine jargon, let us recall the wise words of the great Mark Twain, who once mused, "The human race has only one really effective weapon and that is laughter." With this knowledge firmly planted in our minds and hearts, we stride forth, armed with hilarity and an ever-expanding lexicon, embracing the splendid complexities of wine appreciation and reveling in the eternally evolving landscape of oenophilic humor.

The Grape Divide: Understanding Wine Regions and Their Peculiar Lingo

As our spirited quest to understand the world of wine and its interwoven lexicon continues, we find ourselves standing unwittingly upon the threshold of vast, sprawling vineyards, rolling hills festooned with verdant vines that intoxicate the senses and set one's mind awhirl. For while we previously took pleasure in peeling back the language that attends our oenophilic pursuits, now, we seek to scale the lofty walls of the regions themselves - those hallowed, mysterious territories from whence our most cherished vintages are borne. To merely parse the language of wine is akin to traversing a labyrinth with no walls, whereby our efforts, however valiant, yield a hollow and insubstantial harvest. It is in the living soil, the sun-dappled terrain, and the swirling mists of wine regions that our true quarry resides: an understanding of the peculiar lingo that both illuminates and befuddles our earnest endeavors to comprehend the world of wine.

Inscribed upon this treasured map of ours lie the names of places both celebrated and obscure, leading us ever further down the winding path of regional wine patois. Among the myriad regions that stretch across the globe, we shall unearth the tales of Old World finery and New World vigor, of testaments to the gods themselves inscribed upon parchment worn thin by the hands of history. The shadows of Burgundy, Tuscany, Champagne, and the Douro shall grace our path as we plumb the depths of vinous language, glimpsing the odd phrases and references that resonate and ricochet through innumerable vintages.

Among the winding hills of Burgundy, we encounter the "monopoles" and the "climats" - a veritable lexicon of intrigue and wonder. One might imagine a clandestine board-game of vino swirling about the drawing rooms of the region, pitting connoisseurs against each other in a battle of linguistic wit, as they dexterously parry and thrust with these beguiling terms. Yet beneath the veneer of playfulness lies the solemn truth of Burgundy's terroir-driven identity -- these phrases guiding us towards a deeper understanding of the intricate jigsaw of plots which characterize this storied region.

Venturing further south, we stumble upon the sun-soaked Mediterranean climes of Tuscany, land of the "Super Tuscans." As though plucked from the pages of a superhero comic, these wines leap into our imaginations, flaunting their earth-shaking prowess and unprecedented narrative arcs. One might suspect that these champions of viniculture boast capes of grape leaves and sabers forged from vine wood, and yet the truth is somewhat less fantastical. Super Tuscan wines defy the rigid classifications bestowed upon their brethren, embodying a maverick spirit that scoffs at convention and rules, while delighting on the tongue with equal aplomb.

Our trek through the wine regions of the world continues, as we traverse the hallowed chalk caves of Champagne and delve into a text fraught with undertones of secrecy and surprise. Among all the appellations of the wine world, it is within Champagne that we find the most mesmerizing of contradictions: this realm of glitz and glamour in which prized amber bubbles froth forth from the darkness, illuminating the "riddler" and unveiling the secrets of the "dosage." These are words which evoke echoes of shadowy, candlelit caverns, the hushed whispers of libations shared under a moonless sky - all the while shrouded in an irresistible cloak of ineffable charm and mystique.

As our footsteps echo among the winding valleys of the Douro, we chance upon another curious phrase etched into the fabric of vinous memory: "beneficio." A word steeped in the mysteries of religious tradition, this term is at once a nod to divine providence and arcane ritual, as port vintners imbue their craft with a reverence befitting the holiest of sacraments. It is within the rugged contours of the Douro that we bear witness to the profound union of wine, land, and language, our ever-voracious appetite for idiosyncratic lexicons whetted by the patois of the past.

As we tread the wine-stained timeworn paths of these storied regions, their peculiar lingo slipping seductively from our tongues, we begin to intuit a deeper truth that weaves its way through the very roots and soil of our endeavors. It is in the marriage of the region and its language, its earth and its expression, that the essence of wine ultimately resides - a love affair that transcends time, traversing both the lofty peaks of terroir and the rich tapestry of vinous verbiage. As we embrace this truth, we cannot help but recall the words of the esteemed wine maverick, Hugh Johnson, who once marveled, "The vine reveals its soul in the elements: its earth, convinced; sun, obsessed; air and water, courtiers." Armed with the golden threads of regional wine lingo, may we too ensnare the soul of the vine, and revel in the marvelous and multifaceted world of wine.

Hold Your Tongue: A Wine Newbie's Hilarious Guide to Pronouncing Wine Words

As we embark upon this wine-fueled odyssey of the tongue – a labyrinth of daunting diphthongs, mind-bending brio, and treacherous tongue-twisters – we must throttle our apprehensions and boldly stride forth, our curiosity fortified by the intoxicating elixir that animates our spirits and titillates our senses. For in the hilariously twisted badlands of wine lingo, there exists not only the pitfalls and pratfalls of our linguistic endeavors, but also the opportunity to learn, imbibe, and delight in the wondrous vistas of vino verbiage. And so, dear reader, we raise our glasses in a jubilant toast to the hilarity and humor that awaits, as we set off upon this tongue-in-cheek adventure into the realm of wine words and their oftentimes befuddling pronunciations.

Picture if you will, an ordinary wine-drinking citizen, perhaps – like you – embarking upon their nascent foray into the wonderful world of wine. Clutching a bottle procured from the local supermarket and braced for a joyous evening of gustatory reverie, our intrepid oenophile suddenly finds themselves confounded, flummoxed by the tortuous tangle of letters scrawled upon the label with seeming wanton abandon. Whencefore cometh this conundrum, this merciless miasma of vowels and consonants? Our oft-mispronounced protagonist may well break into a cold sweat at the prospect of uttering such a Gordian knot of nomenclature before friends or at a social event, yet fear not – for in the hilarity that ensues, there exists an opportunity to arm oneself with the knowledge and confidence to confound the snobs and bemuse the skeptics.

First, let us venture to the verdant rolling hills and beguiling terroir of France, where each appellation guards its linguistic treasures with a fervent zeal. Our neophyte wine enthusiasts may curse the day they chose a Grand Cru Classe, ironic that it should be their beloved bottle clutched in trembling hands. The wheezes and splutters that emerge may sound more akin to the death throes of a hitherto unknown, unseen mythical beast than an act of pronouncing this hallowed name, might as well invoke the shadows of a grape-fueled phantasmagoria. Yet, in dismantling the components of the seemingly impenetrable syllables, we find our laughter turning to triumph – as our beleaguered friend discovers that the simple refrain of "grahnd krew klah-say" is not so fearsome after all.

Similarly, our forays into the world of infamous monikers may lead us to encounter the enigmatic Gewürztraminer, its twisted tendrils of consonants ensnaring our unwitting neophyte in a bemused, frantic dance of percussive stammers. In the face of such confounding adversity, we propose, dear reader, a playful mnemonic: think only of the hilarity of "gah-verts-trah-mean-er," as though spoken across a lurching table of inebriated comrades – the inflections of mischief and mirth appended to each syllable.

And what folly would it be to gloss over the alluring, yet oft-mispronounced Pinot Noir? With the fervor of an oenophile adrift among the fog-shrouded vineyards, one may unwittingly twist an "ee" sound into "ay," besmirching the elegant essence of the Pinot with a strangled cry of "pee-noh nwahr." Ah, but heed our cautionary tales and let not your tongue fall victim to such tragic miscues. Instead, softly entreat the "pee-noh n'wah" to spring forth, as smoothly as the delicate raspberry notes that pirouette upon your delighted palate.

As we stumble and bumble our way through the vagaries of the language of wine, let us embrace the folly of farce, and learn to celebrate our mispronunciations with the same gusto as our triumphant articulations. For just as our beloved vino evolves and matures within the dark, cool recesses of the cellar, so too must our oenophilic lexicon develop, enriched by each hilarious misstep and each gleeful burst of laughter. And when at last our wine-infused tongues have been tamed, and our once-awkward stammers give way to a chorus of resplendent elocution, may we in turn raise our glasses high, and toast to the hilarity and the humility that make the process of learning the language of wine not merely an endeavor of the intellect, but a celebration of the heart. For it is in the end, dear reader, not the mastery of esoteric terms that makes our quest for vinous fluency worthwhile, but the inimitable memories and unqualified joy that we share in the company of friends and fellow oenophiles, no matter how we choose to pronounce our cherished libations.

Wine Speak: Playful Interpretations of Wine Descriptions and Tasting Notes

As we venture headlong into the cacophonous carnival of wine lingo that delights and confounds in equal measure, we find ourselves swaddled in the theatrical embrace of wine descriptions and tasting notes. Here amidst the linguistic labyrinth of these swirling phrases, meticulously penned by sommeliers and aficionados the world over, we encounter the unique blend of truth and absurdity that breathes life into the very heart of wine culture. Prepare your palate, fortify your senses, and surrender yourself to the bombastic tumult that is 'Wine Speak' - an exquisite plunge into a whimsical world in which the mundane and the marvelous collide to create, surprisingly, a splash of understanding.

Imagine, if you will, unearthing a tasting note which paints a vinous landscape of "bold currants basking in the midday sun, a chorus of cherries cavorting amidst a susurrus of wet slate and dried lavender." It's as if one has stumbled across an extraterrestrial ecosystem upon removing the cork—an intoxicating, surrealist realm where fruit and flora dance uninhibited alongside geological anomalies. And yet, beneath the veil of playful hyperbole, we begin to perceive the honest intentions of the scribe: a robust, fruit-driven wine with an intriguing mineral backbone and an essence of aromatic flowers woven throughout.

Similarly, we might find ourselves ensorcelled by a swirling maelstrom of meteorological metaphors trapped inside a wine description—a zephyr of zesty zest-ness, a storm of stone fruit, a tempest of tannins that crash like thunder around our beleaguered taste buds. As our imagination frolics among the gusts and gales of this wine-riddled tempest, our logical faculties might question the sanity of such descriptions. And yet, once more, we pry open the elaborate linguistic shell to reveal a hidden pearl of truth: the effervescent, fruit-forward nature of the wine laid bare before us, its tannic structure invigorating rather than intimidating as it awakens our senses with each electric sip.

As we stroll through the verdant gardens of our wine lexicon, we may pause to admire the sprawling landscape of words that lay before us – "buttered toast draped languidly over a honeysuckle hedge, as the mischievous morning mist pirouettes upon the horizon, teasing a Cossack dance between charred oak and apples bathed in sunlight." We find ourselves regaled by a tale of breakfast-time frolics, led on a capricious journey that navigates the borders of possibility and fantasy. Upon closer examination, however, we may discern a tangible thread of meaning woven throughout this extravagant tapestry: the sensual richness of a wine that conjures a delectable brunch scene, its buttery mouthfeel and oaky backbone effortlessly mingling with the pervasive sweetness of ripe apples and the evocative floral notes that hover gently on the palate.

These vivid, evocative musings upon the nature and essence of wine allow us to glimpse the vinous world through magnificently warped and fantastical lenses–the mundane transmuted into something altogether enchanting, something aglow with a mischievous, mercurial energy. By embracing the whimsy and the wit of tasting notes, we may find ourselves unshackling the cumbersome chains of our preconceptions about wine and embarking on a journey of boundless creativity and possibility.

And as we stand arm in arm at the precipice of this new era of delectable perception, casting our glassware aside and leaping into the riotous fray of the wine-splashed page, we recall the wisdom imparted by the erudite poet Alexander Pope: "True ease in writing comes from art, not chance, as those move easiest who have learned to dance." So too, in the realm of Wine Speak, as we swirl and twirl between the piquant imagery, the outlandish similes and the confounding idioms, we discover – unexpectedly – that artfulness, and engage in a mad, joyous dance of our own making. May we remember to embrace the playful complexity of Wine Speak, and allow ourselves the joyful indulgence of a life marked by laughter, libations, and linguistic caprice in equal measure.

Blend It Like a Pro: Crafting Your Own Amusing Wine Lingo

Lo and behold, consider a delightful evening spent with a group of uninformed, yet eager wine drinkers, gathered together in their dedication to the joyous vision vouchsafed by Bacchus himself. They huddle around their mystic elixir, speaking in hushed and reverential tones as one gently lifts its lunar notes to one's nostrils, another detects the whispers of an ocean breeze upon one's lips, and yet another detects a hint of the ethereal effervescence that has long since vanished from mortal ken. However, it is not the lyrical waxings of these awed neophytes that baffle and bemuse our highly trained, intellectually enigmatic sommelier protagonist – rather, it is the absence of any referencing to the classic wine phraseology, or, in simpler terms, the artsy-fartsy, jargon-filled prose that has defined the world of wine-speak. But fear not, for our erudite epicurean will seize the opportunity to teach the vinous greenhorns how they might find delight in stretching their imaginative faculties to their utmost extremes.

We begin with a primer on the complexities of acidity – that zesty element which cuts through our favorite wines like a verdant sorbet, tingling one's precious buds into vibrant life. With a persuasive wiggle of one's brows, one might encourage the inexperienced imbiber to describe the slings and arrows of incisive acidity in an imaginative way, such as "dancing mandarins juggling blades," ever closer and closer to the precipice of one's tongue. Thus begins the rollicking journey toward linguistic invention, where each new phrase – however ridiculous it may seem – becomes a stepping-stone toward a pantheon of one's own making.

Likewise, as one ventures from the beautiful vistas of crisp, effervescent wines into the charred, toast-laden climes of oak-driven libations, it is not enough for one to simply waffle on about tannins and barrique-aging. Instead, aspire to inject a sense of playfulness into it, summoning forth awe-inspiring metaphors like "a roaring bonfire that lingers within the hearth of one's soul" – a foolproof method to evoke the soul-nourishing warmth offered by such libations.

It is essential as well, as we sip daintily from our chalices, to consider the role of fruit and floral elements in our amusing lingo. Instead of dullfully describing the sensation of devouring berries and orchard fruits, one might envision, say, a surrealist painting of strawberries and cherries waltzing merrily among the lilacs and roses in a fertile garden of bountiful delights. Such language may at first glance baffle and confound one's intellect, but on deeper examination, it serves as a lantern, guiding the intrepid explorer to reach a lush and vivid understanding of the wine's very essence.

Amidst all this, dear reader, let not the process of inventing one's own wine lingo discourage thee. For it is in embracing the inherent silliness and the tongue-in-cheek artistry of it that we free ourselves from the solemn shackles of oenologic pedantry, allowing our imaginations to run wild and our laughter to rise unchecked. The clash of flavors, textures, and bouquets conjured through outlandishly amusing descriptions will not only entertain and enlighten fellow wine enthusiasts but, perhaps most importantly, empower thyself to look beyond the veil of pompous pretentiousness to find the heart and soul of the sacred libation you hold in your hands.

So, as we raise our glasses to the heavens, toasting not only to our vinous triumphs but to the boundless joy of linguistic creation, let us embrace the singular union of word and wine that has brought us thus far. Let us acknowledge and celebrate the fact that, while bubble and bouquet may wax and wane, the power of the spoken word remains ever our steadfast companion, our guiding light in the ongoing quest to extract the maximum enjoyment from every facet of our lives – not the least of which is the mysterious, ethereal, and breathtakingly divine realm of wine within which we so willingly immerse ourselves, again and again.

Talking Tipsy: Using Wine Lingo to Impress Friends and Confuse Snobs

With an enigmatic gleam in our eyes and a devilish grin upon our lips, let us embark upon the deliriously exciting journey of Talking Tipsy: the art of confounding snobbery with the arsenal of wine lingo at our disposal. As we wade through the swirling vernacular sea, let us tease forth the precious pearls that lurk beneath the surface, waiting to be plucked like a lyre and strung into a symphony of effervescent amusement. With stealth and cunning, we shall weave a tapestry of linguistic deception that will delight, confuse, and impress; as we hold aloft our chalices of inebriated intellect, it is our mission, nay, our sworn duty, to disarm the snobbish sentinels with the rapier-like wit of wine lingo.

Let us begin our dastardly exploits by turning our attention toward the mysterious realm of "mouthfeel." This oft-overlooked aspect of wine-speak might be casually tossed aside by the uninitiated as a trivial detail, but those with even a modicum of wisdom know that it is here that some of the most deliciously devilish phrases can be coaxed from the very heart of the grape. Picture, for example, the furrowing of our sophisticated opponent's brow as we nonchalantly refer to the wine as "an elegantly choreographed Bolshoi ballet pirouetting across an abandoned velvet ballroom." The implications of such a description are numerous and beguiling – and as our adversary searches fruitlessly for logical meaning in our words, a pang of frenetic doubt may blossom within them.

Or perhaps our devious hearts may lead us down a more geological path, as we employ the language of the elements themselves to craft a villainous web of confusion. Might we not speak of a wine that boasts "a overtly volcanic nature, with the simmering tectonic plates of tropical fruit and heady, dark chocolate gradually yielding to a triumphant eruption of smoky cinders" – a tumultuous cataclysm trapped within the bounds of our very glass? We may pause for effect, allowing the mingling of geological calamity and enological splendor to weave their bewildering spell upon those who dare challenge our wine-related prowess.

Having solidified our position amid the lofty pinnacles of wine lingo, we may then proceed to unleash the most labyrinthine of olfactory descriptions in order to further bewitch and beguile. Consider, friends, the simpering fanfare that may erupt as we speak of "inhaling the sultry, swirling essence of a dried Comoros dance upon a trembling cloud of Macedonian pears poached in moonlight, as they lock eyes in a passionate embrace with the distant specters of Sahara rain and Oaxacan chocolate." Like a Neapolitan perfume factory run amok, we toss forth a bouquet of unlikely and intriguing aromas that waft through the ethers of our companion's comprehension, prompting a symphony of confusion and delight to play upon their furrowed brows.

Our pièce de résistance, however, comes not from the mellifluous minuets of metaphors nor the ambrosial amalgamations that lend themselves to our rampant linguistic contortions. Rather, our zenith lies in the ability to weave a golden thread of ambiguity throughout our carefully-chosen threads of wine lingo – to inject an element of uncertainty that leaves our listeners questioning not only the veracity of our words, but the very foundation of their most sacrosanct beliefs. In doing so, we unveil the ultimate weapon of Talking Tipsy: the poetic paradox.

When we speak reverentially of a wine that "invites the soul to dance with the first rays of a nascent sunrise, whilst simultaneously plunging us into the inky depths of a bleak, impenetrable darkness," we shroud ourselves in an impregnable cloak of unanswerable queries. As our companions stutter and stumble in their futile attempts to grasp the elusive truths that dance tantalizingly away from their clammy fingertips, we smile inwardly and know that we have succeeded – for Talking Tipsy is a dance where victory is measured not by the clarity of our words, but by the riotous, joyous chaos they leave in their wake.

As we sip the lingering essence of our successes, we might reflect upon how ingenious deployment of wine-speak may offer surprising insights into the human condition. Caught between the conflicting realities of gravity and effervescence, of shadow and light, we pause a moment to consider the delight that lies in the corners of contradiction – and resolve to carry this newfound appreciation with us, as we continue our odyssey through the glorious paradoxes of vinous vernacular. And so, with a twinkle in our eye, we bid adieu to the snobs we have confounded and the friends we have impressed, saluting the hilarity and creativity of Talking Tipsy, as we stride forth with a renewed appetite for life, love, and laughter.

Witty Wine Pairings: Comic Combinations for Every Occasion

What do I need as well?

And so, we begin our journey with a heady, tipsy toe-dip into the madcap realm of first-date frenzy, where the lines between gastronomic delicacies and romantic disaster blur and shimmer like the edges of sun-drenched dreams. Picture the scene: two strangers, sharing a tentative candlelit dinner as they tentatively navigate the great wine list of love. Our well-intentioned protagonist, driven by the desire to impress his dining companion, chooses an unlikely pairing of a lusciously sweet Sauternes – typically reserved for foie gras or crème brûlée – with a steaming serving of spicy Thai curry. The result? A riotous explosion of sweet heat that sets tongues wagging and eyebrows arching faster than you can say "wine faux pas."

Meanwhile, perhaps we have a merry band of friends gathered for a casual backyard barbecue, glasses clinking and laughter echoing beneath an azure sky. As whimsy takes hold, our host joyously introduces the unlikely pairing of a hearty, smoky Malbec with the creaminess of ham salad – a gastronomic collision that spins off course into a comic tornado of flavors, where culinary worlds collide with unexpected hilarity.

Next, as the sun sinks slowly behind the horizon and the cold, neon glow of city lights flicker to life, we find another delightful duo hunched over a rickety table in their cozy, dimly lit abode – their hearts warmed by the presence of hot, steaming takeout and the glow of their shared affection. What could be more riotous than daring to pair a delicate, ethereal Pinot Noir with the greasy goodness of a salt-streaked package of fish and chips? As the tales of this unlikely double act spread, a motley crew of gastronomes and gourmands may cluck their tongues in disapproval, but our intrepid diners understand that, amidst the laughter that follows the unpredictable convergence of wine and deep-fried cuisine, an unexpected gastric symphony is waiting to be sung.

As we wend our way through the dizzying global landscape of wine, we must naturally turn our attention to the cacophonous symphony of cultural collisions that brims with amusing wine pairings whose sole purpose is to baffle and bemuse our palates. Picture, if you will, the stiff-upper-lipped realm of quintessential English afternoon tea, complete with dainty sandwiches, diminutive pastries, and — in a daring play — a generous splash of a bold, full-bodied Barolo, whose vibrant tannins and intense, dark fruits threaten to usurp the delicate trinity of cucumber, Earl Grey, and scone (lest we forget the clotted cream). A more unorthodox match could scarcely be imagined, yet it is in the very absurdity of this pairing that we are left giggling behind our raised pinkies, an amused gleam in our eyes.

Finally, we come to the grand finale of this madcap culinary cáca milis: the bubbling, effusive glories of sparkling wine, and the comic combinations that lie therein. What could be more entertaining than chasing a robust Irish stew with the effervescent charm of Prosecco, or nibbling daintily at sushi while sipping a zesty Cava? In these playback pairings, we find the permission to laugh, to embrace the absurdist nature of life, and to push the boundaries of our gastronomic understanding - all with a twinkle of mischief in our eyes.

As we bid farewell to this topsy-turvy tableau of unconventional wine pairings, it is our fervent hope that, armed with this newfound knowledge and an irrepressible sense of humor, we may continue our gastronomic adventures with the wry wit and jocund abandon that accompanies the very best of vinous delights. Must we forever cleave to the mundane, the expected, the trite? Surely not, dear friends, when a world of Bratwurst and Beaujolais, Malort and macarons, lie just beyond the horizon of our collective culinary consciousness. And so, with our appetites whetted, our spirits buoyed, and our tastebuds trembling with equal parts excitement and trepidation, let us sally forth into the great unknown, all the while raising a cheers to the unparalleled joy and sheer, unadulterated hilarity of unconventional wine pairings - be they real or imagined, successful or disastrous, hallowed or banished into the realm of myth and legend.

First-date Frenzies: Hysterical Pairings for Romantic Beginnings

As we embark upon the thrilling journey of gastronomic discovery and romance, let us raise a glass to the capricious and unpredictable world of first-date frenzy, where passions are kindled and doused, dreams are formed and shattered, and the unsuspecting palate is subjected to a carnival of unconventional – and often uproarious – wine pairings. In this brave new world of impulsive decision-making and gastronomic whimsy, we shall peer beneath the lace-trimmed veneer of elegance and eloquence, and plunge head-first into the swirling vortex of delightfully disastrous matchups that shall forevermore serve as both a warning and an amusement for those with the courage to brave the high seas of culinary matrimony.

Ah, dear friends, imagine the sweet serendipity of a first encounter, where nervous laughter mingles with the intoxicating aromas of a shared repast, and navigation through the perplexing maze of romantic expectations is – at last! – nearing its much-anticipated denouement. Surely, it is here that the fickle finger of fate – keen to lend a touch of comic whimsy to proceedings – inspires a quixotic selection of Malbec, with its robust, earthy undertones, to share intimate quarters with a brace of lightly poached eggs, glistening coyly beneath their blanket of hollandaise sauce? Gently, we shall allow the explosive combination of rich tannins and velvety cream to echo the adventure and uncertainty of this fledgling liaison, their clash a reminder that even opposites can conspire to delight, if only for an ephemeral moment.

And, as the warm embrace of an evening casts its seductive spell, we might turn to the languid, honeyed caress of a voluptuous Gewürztraminer and its delectable dance with the sharp, bracing tang of a delicately tart citrus ceviche. In this incongruous pas de deux, the merry-go-round of sweet, spicy, and sour shares the spotlight with the thrilling, uneasy waltz of attraction and apprehension. A bead of perspiration gleaming upon the brow, a quiver of anticipation – these twin sensations shall serve as both a testament to the unexpected power of a playful wine pairing and an exclamation mark upon the unfolding narrative of love's halting first steps.

As the evening unfolds, wine-soaked conversations taking flight like a fleet of intoxicated doves, our amorous protagonists may choose to explore the sweet mysteries that lie at the heart of the mouthfeel. Let us consider, for example, the transporting sensation when a tart Chenin Blanc is introduced to its culinary counterpart in the form of a plate heaped high with sizzling barbecue ribs, resplendent in their sticky, saucy glory. The entreaties of acidity may press against the temptation of caramel notes, a duel of pleasure and laughter filling the air with joyful peals of mirth as our blushing daters encounter the revelation of gastronomic discord and unity.

Each unconventional pairing serves as a tart reminder of life's tangled webs – both on the plate and in the realm of amour – and as we raise a toast to these merry misadventures, we may choose to reflect upon the beauty of imperfection, of serendipity, and of the sheer, triumphant chaos that reigns when first-date wine pairings are embraced with both passion and humor. For it is in these gleeful incompatibilities, where flavor, texture, and aroma tumble and pirouette to the music of inspired eccentricity, that we uncover a hidden truth: life, love, and indeed wine, are richer and more rewarding when filled with moments that defy logic, and that coax smiles from those who dare to dream.

So, as we navigate the labyrinthine pathways of the human heart, arm in arm with our co-conspirators in gastronomic rebellion, let us hold fast to the lessons that amusing wine pairings impart: to seek joy in the unexpected, to cherish the beauty of spontaneity, and to embrace quirky combinations as the lifeblood of our romantic exploits. For in the unfathomable dance of fate lies the promise of a mirthful, memorable, and unforgettable evening, steeped in laughter, roguish charm, and a cascade of novel encounters that enrich our senses, our memories, and ultimately, our very souls.

Cracking up at Casual Gatherings: Unexpected Wine Matches for your Backyard BBQ

As we venture beyond the dew-tinged landscapes of romantic first forays into the gustatory unknown, we must now steel our palates for the rollicking carnival that is the casual gathering: that jovial tableau of camaraderie, laughter, and the subtle alchemy of flame and flavor that transforms humble cuts of meat and simple vegetables into a veritable feast. Amidst the sizzle of sausages, the crackle of coals, and the triumphant plumes of fragrant, billowing smoke, we shall now turn our attention to the dizzying world of unconventional wine pairings, fully embracing the riotous potential that such endeavors hold for delighting the senses and inciting roars of laughter from even the most jaded of backyard gourmands.

Picture the scene: a merry band of friends and family, gathered beneath the dappled shade of a sprawling oak tree, the air alive with snatches of conversation and gusts of hearty laughter. At the heart of this convivial milieu, the flames of the barbecue dance and lick at the succulent offerings that lie smoldering upon the grill. It is in this setting that we shall frolic with the motley crew of oddball wine inclusions, choosing to defy the conventional strictures of culinary wisdom in the name of revelry and the sweet succor of the unexpected.

First up, we shall greet the ever-delectable steak, its rich, juicy depths seared to perfection and aching for release. Eschewing the traditional embrace of a robust Cabernet Sauvignon or a smoky Shiraz, our brave hosts instead unveil the startling visage of an ice-cold Albariño, its crisp, zesty notes a veritable splash of citrus upon the tongue. As we watch the company's collective eyebrows take flight, it is with a sly, sidelong smile that we indulge in this improbable union, savoring the thrill of scandal as the duet of flavors pirouette and collide, their shared dance one of carnivalesque charm and temptation.

As the evening wears on and the strains of laughter ripple through the air like the sweetest strains of a symphony, our thoughts turn to the delights yet to be discovered amidst the trove of unpredictable pairings. A platter of lovely flame-kissed vegetables tiptoes into view, their sedate flavors surely ripe for the pairing with a light and sprightly white - or so they might have us believe! In a flash of gastronomic whimsy, our intrepid hosts unveil an unsuspecting Pinotage, those smoky, earthy notes chortling with glee as they join forces with the roasted charm of the vegetables – a harmony of triumphant weirdness.

Our appetites momentarily satiated, we may turn our attention to one of the ubiquitous stars of the backyard barbecue, reserving its position in the hearts and stomachs of many: the humble hot dog. Laden with the neon glow of relish, the twinkle of mustard, and the earthy allure of sauerkraut, this frankfurter fiesta is surely a worthy foil for the sparkling effervescence of a lighthearted Lambrusco. Together, they form a culinary double-act that delights and bemuses in equal measure, their mutual sense of absurdity perfectly matched as the transition from condiment-laden treat to celebratory quaff triggers a cascade of giggles from those who dare to indulge.

With each unlikely pairing – be it smoky Riesling with barbecued chicken, or the winsome chime of Viognier as it pirouettes gracefully around a platter of slow-cooked pulled pork – we reaffirm the spirit of abandon and mirth that lies at the core of our collective culinary adventures. It is in embracing the idiosyncrasies, the frivolous dalliances, and the headlong collisions of the palate that we rekindle within ourselves the spirit of playfulness, tantalizing our imaginations with the sheer, unadulterated thrill of the unorthodox.

As the sun sinks into the horizon and leaves a twilight glow in its wake, it is our fervent hope that the laughter and amusement that accompanied our backyard barbecue – and the madcap array of unexpected wine pairings that colored its progression – will serve as a reminder to us all of the ephemeral joys and fleeting chimeras that flavor the fabric of our lives. At the close of day, the fire may have been extinguished, and the last toast raised, but the memories of our audacious adventure into the realm of improbable culinary unions shall linger long after the charcoal has cooled and the sound of laughter has fallen silent in the night. And so, inspired by the thrill of the unexpected, we may all raise our glasses to the joy, the wonder, and the unending delight of the unconventional wine pairing, a vibrant thread within the tapestry of those playful, light-hearted evenings that defy convention, but define our very spirit.

Hilarity at Home: Laughing over Wine and Takeout Combinations

As we navigate our way through the vibrant, bustling landscape of daily life – adorned as it is with all manner of sensory delights and distractions – there are few pleasures as universally beloved or eagerly anticipated as that moment when the doorbell chimes, heralding the arrival of our revered sustenance: the takeout meal. As we peel back the steam-soaked layers of aluminum foil and styrofoam, our hearts flutter with anticipation and our taste buds tremble with expectation at the bountiful feast that lies within. Indeed, few pastimes lend themselves quite as aptly to both the sophisticated palate and the whimsical heart as the act of pairing wine with takeout, each union a delightful cavalcade of culinary whimsy that serves as both a tribute to the joyful potential of gastronomic adventure and a celebration of life's simplest, chain-jangling pleasures.

Imagine, if you will, the pleasing sight of your favorite sushi platter, resplendent in its Lilliputian magnificence – the gleaming coral hues of salmon sashimi nestled artfully alongside the opalescent glow of pillows of sticky rice draped elegantly with translucent, buttery folds of meltingly tender tuna. The customary accompaniment of soy sauce and delightfully potent wasabi, of course, beckons us to quaff a fragrant, crisp white wine brimming with the tang of citrus and the whisper of snow-melted mountain streams. And yet, it is within the realm of the unexpected that we uncover the full kaleidoscope of hilarity: instead of said white wine, a cheerful bottle of Chianti is unceremoniously thrust into the spotlight, the robust chorus of tannins and ripe cherry notes jostling for center stage as they playfully engage with the delicate symphony of umami and fish-oil that graces the sushi morsels. An uproarious pas de deux of the palate, this improbable pairing sets a mirthful tone for the evening's festivities, ensuring that no platter of takeout sushi shall ever glow with quite the same luminous hue of preposterous possibility henceforth.

As if emboldened by this spirited display of impromptu matchmaking, our hearts turn now toward another beloved denizen of the weeknight hankering: the joyous jumble of spice, char, and fragrant herbs that is Indian takeout. Bejeweled with glistening pools of oil, the great continents of cumin and turmeric-laden gravies, studded with a cornucopia of chili – both fresh and dried – is enough to set ablaze the spirit of gastronomic mischief within even the most jaded of food adventurers. The conventional choice, of course, would be the tried and tested Gewürztraminer – the noble emissary of the Alsatian vineyards – whose unctuous, honeyed voluptuousness is an antidote to the flames that dance upon the tongue. But instead, as is our wont, we plunge with gleeful abandon toward the unknown and the unsanctioned, opting for the unbridled vivacity of a South African Sauvignon Blanc. Conjure, if you will, the thrill of savoring the vigorous interplay of green pepper and gooseberry as they engage in irreverent discourse with a tongue-searing vindaloo – a feat of culinary derring-do that will leave friends and family agog with disbelief, but full of admiration for our bold, innovative choice.

As our gastronomic tour of takeout classics reaches its zenith, it is only fitting that we pay homage to the humble, yet deeply emotive, world of comfort food. Picture the scene, then: a table laden with all the trappings of culinary cosiness – from the molten depths of a rich, creamy potato gratin, to the glistening, golden-brown landscape of a well-executed mac and cheese – each dish a paean to the soothing balm of indulgent nostalgia, and a reminder of the unique power of food to lift our spirits and unite us in the heady embrace of solace and sanctuary. It may be here that we choose to conclude our delightful adventure into the chaotic world of wine and takeout combinations, opting for a slyly acerbic twist by selecting a sweet, unctuous dessert wine to counteract the richness of those toasted crumb toppings. The gleeful fizz of a refreshing Moscato d'Asti, perhaps, with its delicate rasp of peach fuzz and tantalizing sparkle, can shake hands with the homely charms of beef bourguignon or shepherd's pie, creating a marriage of blissful quirkiness that soars above the twin realms of expectation and mundane reality.

In celebrating the hilarity of these unlikely unions – where the boundaries of tradition and expectation are gleefully disregarded in favor of the sweet art of the absurd – we rekindle within ourselves the very essence of human curiosity and creativity, using the humble act of wine pairing as a conduit for exploring not just the intricate landscape of the palate and the senses, but also the allegorical riches that lie deep within the human soul. And thus, we may find ourselves embarking upon a far more potent journey – one that enraptures not only our taste buds but also beckons us to embrace the boundless capacity for joy, laughter and wonder that lies dormant within each and every one of us. With each bite of takeout and sip of wine, we unlock the secrets of the universe, illuminating the ever-widening pathways of the cosmos with the flickering flames of life, love, and laughter.

Bridging Cultural Comedies: Humorous Global Pairings to Satisfy Your Wanderlust

As we cast our gaze upon the sun-smeared horizon, the thundering crescendo of heavy suitcases and crumpled itineraries filling the air, it is with the spirit of the intrepid explorer and the mischievous gourmand that we sally forth into the wildly unpredictable realm of global wine pairings. Indeed, few endeavors are imbued with such boundless potential for both laughter and edification as that peculiar alchemical collision between cultures, the errant fireworks of flavor and tradition igniting our senses as we gleefully cavort with chaos in the name of hedonistic pleasure.

Picture this: the steaming, fragrant whirlwind of the Souk – a bustling Moroccan marketplace where the very air is suffused with a kaleidoscope of exotic spices, their heady aromas trailing behind the haphazard procession of colorful kaftans and clattering carts. It is here that we encounter our first marvellous collision of cross-cultural tongue tingling, in the form of the ubiquitous lamb tagine – its rich, sensuous depths brimming with slow-cooked meats and perfume-laden fruits, a symphony of tangled flavors and shimmering textures that mesmerize the tongue and bewitch the senses. In defiance of expectations, we choose to pair this perplexing treasure not with the suave, dusky charms of a well-traveled Bordeaux or a velvety Californian Merlot, but with the cool silk of a South Korean soju, its hot fuselage of fleeting fire a supernatural counterpoint to the soothing balm of the tagine's intoxicating depths. As we bid farewell to the winding, shadowy warrens of the bazaar, it is in the warmth of the evening sun that we remind ourselves that the beauty of laughter lies not in the mirror of a shared echo, but also in the shining revelation of pure unadulterated whimsy.

Soothed by the fiery embrace of soju and the shimmering melody of Moroccan spices, our globetrotting taste buds next alight upon the sleepy shores of the Mediterranean – the sun-dappled cradle of a cuisine that is both nurturing and steeped in the hallowed traditions of antiquity. Dare to frolic, then, with the kaleidoscope of botantically bedecked wonders that adorn the pebbled streets of a Greek taverna. Fingers slick with the remnants of anointment by fragrant olive oil, we turn our attention to the ubiquitous fish platter –that symphony of delicate flavors, rendered translucent by the gentlest flickerings of fire and flame. Behold the hero of this Mediterranean escapade: a fine Australian Cabernet Sauvignon, treasured for its tannins and the ability to pair with hearty red meats. And with cheeks flushed and poised for laughter, we tear asunder the very fabric of the tannic straitjacket that constricts our sense of humor – the crimson song now recast as a delicious foil for the brazen subtleties of charred fish, slicked with vibrant green olive oil and marinated with the tenderness and care of a thousand and one sunsets.

With the intoxicating memory of that first riotous tryst still lingering like a half-remembered ghost, we turn our wanderlust-fueled senses now to the last outpost of our sojourn amongst the world's culinary wilderness: the bustling thoroughfares of Mexico. Bathed in the colors of a thousand sunsets, our steps are guided by the twang of guitar strings, their melodies inexorably intertwined with the rich symphony of spice, smoke, and earth that is the birthright and lifeblood of this rich and vibrant nation. The serenade of fire and passion that accompanies a plate of carnitas – delicate shreds of slow-simmered and deeply caramelized pork, encased within the soft, pliant embrace of a fresh tortilla – beguiles both heart and palate, leading us into humorous abandon as we shun the customary callings of a smoky mezcal or the crisp, amber serenade of a chilled Mexican lager. Instead, an impossibly pale and ethereal Vinho Verde from Portugal rises to meet our culinary daredevilry, its effervescent, verdant zest a waltzing partner to the earthy allure of the carnitas, and our laughter – a spiral of sound and color ascending toward the heavens.

As we return, sated and inebriated, to the shores of familiarity and tradition, it is with a sense of embracing defiance that we raise glass to the riotous adventure we have embarked upon, celebrating the improbable unions forged not just in the name of gastronomic delight, but in the pursuit of laughter and cross-cultural understanding. In this sun-kissed, vine-entwined world of feasting and folly, the wineglass is no longer a vessel of sober reflection, but a chalice brimming with the elixir of joy and healing. United as a cherished old friend and a forlorn stranger alike under the wistful banner of a shared global tongue, we take the first tentative steps toward a world that is nourished by laughter, warmed by the bonfire of a thousand disparate hearts, and where the heady perfume of untold culinary alliances is as universal a balm as the soothing strains of a gypsy lullaby.

Bubbly Belly Laughs: Sparkling Wine Pairings for a Cheerful Celebration

At the zenith of lighthearted merrymaking and convivial cheer, we find ourselves drawn, like moths to the enchanting glow of laughter, toward a libation that has delighted and stupefied humankind for centuries: sparkling wine. For who among us can truly resist the allure of those tiny, liquid-born pearls, the shimmering harbinger of fun that dances merrily within the confines of a fluted glass like the very incarnation of happiness itself? It is in the spirit of puckish joy that we now turn our attention to the art of pairing these beguiling elixirs with food, their combined effervescence a lighthearted accompaniment to an evening of laughter and reminiscence, a shared titter and a rousing guffaw alike.

Picture this: a sumptuous banquet, groaning under the weight of dishes both sublime in their elegance and mischievous in their assault on tradition. A whisper of freshly shucked oysters, their pearly wings poised in mid-flight, lies nestled among the maelstrom of treats, the earthly scent of a pantomime of fungi – magnificent in its multicolored splendor – wafting seductively in the air like a velvet curtain about to be drawn. The conventional choice of libation, of course, would be an exquisite and venerable Champagne; but eschewing the soothing hum of familiarity, we elect to pair this culinary escapade with a quixotic interloper from the rugged shores of Tasmania. As the emerald liquid within the bottle fizzes and bubbles against the vibrant flavors of the oyster and the heady aroma of the mushrooms, it is as if the air itself is alight with laughter, the very molecules of flavor conspiring to create a symphony that unleashes the intoxicating melodies of mirth and whimsy.

Emboldened by the unorthodox and subversive possibilities of such pairings, we venture gleefully into the realm of the absurd, striding intrepidly toward the perfumed orbit of the Thai curry – a moody, brooding concoction whose soulful embrace sparks a fever within the heart of the glutton. Logic might dictate that the complex tapestry of flavors contained within such intricate creations is best matched by the cool, placid embrace of a crisp white wine. And yet, as if in revolt against the tyrannical clutches of convention and prosaic mundanity, we instead opt for a lively and blithe Spanish Cava, its ebullient leaps of peach, apple, and citrus notes sweeping around the tongue like a flock of helium balloons soaring mysteriously skyward. The joyous interplay between the delicate symphony of the curry and the rambunctious cacophony of the Cava is a chorus that imbues each exultant mouthful with the propulsive harmony of unadulterated gaiety.

Our journey through the whimsical universe of sparkling wine pairings would, of course, be incomplete without a nod to the mischievous trickster harbored within the heart of every sommelier – the gleeful apprehension that ignites their very souls as they recount their most unlikely escapades and dastardly victories. As dusk blossoms into nightfall, and the laughter worth a hundred suns begins to wane, we pause to savor one final sparkling concoction that is equal parts audacious, innovative, and bafflingly brilliant. A dessert, festooned with the gold of ripened citrus and the amber of caramel, demands a partner that can both match and underscore its unapologetic wealth of sweetness. Enter, then, the redoubtable Italian Lambrusco, its lustrous ruby sheen and resolute profile a visage of good-natured defiance as it giggles along with the saccharine tunes of crème brûlée or lemon tart, a swooning waltz of fruit, sugar, and delectably vivacious froth.

As the final notes of that exuberant dance fade on the tongue, and the echoes of laughter recede into the hazy, twilight realms of memory, we are left with a sense of satisfaction derived not just from the symphony of flavors that has graced our palates, but also from the electrifying thrill of departing from the well-trodden path of convention. In leaping headlong into the zany universe of sparkling wine pairings, we have embraced the potential for new adventures, for even greater feats of culinary derring-do, armed with little more than our sense of humor and a willingness to laugh in the face of gastronomic norms. It is in this spirit of levity and defiance that we drink to the future, to a world where the delightful cacophony of sparkling wine pairings intertwines forevermore with the sweet elixir of laughter, the eternal golden threads of joy and revelry that bind us all in the spirit of unbounded celebration and discovery.

Etiquette and Amusing Misadventures: Wine Faux Pas and Social Sipping

No matter how many times you mess up. Stay strong and find your own taste ;-)

There exists, in the heady, intoxicating world of wine, a fine line between the glittering heights of social grace and the vertiginous plunge into ungainly disaster, a treacherous tightrope that all too often leaves its victims stranded, suspended in an abyss of their own blushing mortification. Yet, for those who possess the resilience to traverse these fraught, humor-slicked lengths with grace and charisma, there lies in store an unmatched reward: the thrill of mastering the minutiae of wining etiquette and the opportunity to delight, amuse, and educate in equal measure.

Let us begin our awkward odyssey toward the heart of the social sipping faux pas with an image as old as time itself: the hapless would-be bon vivant, their unsteady fingers trembling beneath the burden of a wayward corkscrew, its tip skittering and dancing across the evasive surface of the stubborn cork; a spectacle that leaves onlookers wincing in sympathy and not-altogether-well-disguised amusement. Picture, now, the inevitable conclusion of this ill-fated endeavor: the tortured heart-rending *pop*, as the hapless victim frees their quarry amid a tumult of soggy cork shrapnel and airborne wine droplets, the besmirched offering now sullying the pristine innocence of a once-proud stemware. With laughter tinging the air like the biting scent of tragedy's own perfume, it is in this moment of ignominy that we boldly embrace the undeniable truth: the art of uncorking has the power to plunge the unwary, the ungainly, and the undeterred alike into depths of hilarity and discomfort.

For the fearless seek to sup with giants, we must surmount the chalice-heavy gauntlet of wine glass etiquette – that molten core of disaster that lurks, and waits, and bides its time in the unsuspecting fingers of the neophyte, waiting, like a coiled snake, to strike. A glass, held too firmly, too high, or too low, may elicit the same despairing sigh, the raise of an eyebrow in resigned exasperation, but an unsteady grip or an ill-timed flourish could mean the ruination of an otherwise delightful evening. With laughter teetering in the wings, our heroic wine enthusiasts must parry the perilous feints of errant stemware, avoiding the proverbial soufflé of embarrassment that rises, unseen, like the fabled Kraken, to engulf its hapless victims.

As if the quagmire of potential humiliation that comprises the ritual of corkscrewing and stemware were not sufficiently chasmic, the wine lover must also stretch themselves to traverse the minefield of aeration, that slippery, serpentine beast that first rears its monstrous head in the form of a decanter – its purpose clear, its use less so. Grasped with unsteady hands, the wine sloshes like a petulant tempest within its crystal confines, bidding escape and freedom with the maniacal zeal of an anarchist. Reaching its crescendo amid the childish flecks of laughter that do little to ease the discomfort of its unfortunate architect, the decanter finally delivers its coup de grâce: a tumultuous outpouring of wine that stains and drowns its surroundings in reckless abandon, leaving its chief orchestrator to dwell in a new-found gloom so exquisitely profound that it seems to rival even the cheer of peacocks in the sun.

From the jumble of instincts, memories, and whispered advice that comprise the concatenations of wine etiquette, there are those that evoke an unrivaled chorus of laughter and mirth: the noise created by the act of sniffing wine, that delicate art of inhaling the ethereal perfume of vinous bliss that can, in the inexperienced hands of the neophyte, take on a timbre so at odds with its intended purpose - stilling the flow of conversation and eliciting a barely-suppressed cacophony of chortling and hilarity. As innocent as the act may seem, it can be fraught with challenge, demanding an almost superhuman level of pluck and finesse from its practitioner, lest they find themselves permanently enshrined in the unofficial gallery of bacchanalian hijinks.

Swirling, the pièce de résistance in this gallery of hilarity, poses perhaps the most potent threat to the unwary wine amateur – its siren call summoning eager, unsteady fingers and a wealth of misguided confidence as it sends forth its omnipotent tempest of chaos. From the elegant gentle rotation of a glass poised at an angle worthy of feasting royalty, to the ungodly vortex that sends wine spewing forth from its chalice as if liberated from the uncaring tyranny of the bottle that has caged it for so long.

The parade of faux pas and mishaps that bedeck the wine-soaked gatherings of humankind are as numerous as the stars, their brilliance illuminating and magnifying the ungainly, the awkward, and the mortified in equal measure. Yet, in their often merciless grip, we find a unifying bond, a common thread that weaves us together into a tapestry of shared experience and eccentricity.

As we untangle and extricate ourselves from the dizzying world of wine faux pas and social sipping, it can be tempting to dwell in the bittersweet memory of unrequited dreams of etiquette mastery. But it is in the twinkle of a knowing smile, the chuckle shared between friends, or the soft gravitas of a knowing nod that we find solace: as we share our tales of blunder, this shared humor, this essential and unshakeable link that allows us to share our amusements and our peccadilloes with unfiltered warmth. For in the tapestry of laughter, clumsiness threads its way, enriching its vigor and binding it to a mosaic of unforgettable vignettes that at once startle, astonish, and humiliate – a testament to the indomitable power of human inebriation.

Uncorking Catastrophes: Hilarious Tales of Opening Wine Bottles Wrongly

The carnage wrought by a seemingly innocuous wine bottle is, in truth, a malady as old as the invention of wine itself: a tableau of tragedy and amusement that has painted the cheeks of generations of unfortunate victims with the rosy hue of unbidden laughter, born of frustration, confusion, or sheer, undiluted exasperation. And yet, within this miasma of amusing misadventures, perhaps no catastrophe is quite so deserving of our sympathetic, if mirthful, attention than the debacle of an uncorking gone disastrously awry – a phenomenon that, by virtue of its ubiquity, has ascended to the lofty heights of urban legend and cemented itself within the annals of humorous, wine-fueled lore.

To truly understand the comical maelstrom of a flummoxed uncorking, we must consider the countless diverse and wit-rich scenarios that pervade the minds of those present, like spectators to a performance where art and folly collide in a crescendo of vivid, surreal tableaux. As we survey the multitude of human encounters with stubborn corks, each fraught with frustration and comedy, we are confronted with a dazzling array of ignominious misadventures, from the novice sommelier seeking to impress on their first date to the overzealous and injudicious enthusiast who wreaks havoc upon a wedding celebration and the hapless, middle-aged work colleague who finds themselves at the whims of their corporate taskmasters as their manic yet earnest attempts to uncork the forlorn beverage before them descends into a farce, best watched from a safe distance.

Let us begin with the classic cautionary tale – the first date, a scenario etched in time since the very dawn of human courtship, and as varied in detail and nuance as the stars in the pantheon of romantic escapades. Our protagonist, with eyes brimming with hope and the faintest glimmer of vulnerability, is faced with the ultimate challenge: meeting high expectations while remaining endearingly unique, with the added challenge of operating a corkscrew, a formidable foe to be sure. As the carefully extracted cork plunges into the liquid depths below with a disheartening splash, the whispers of effervescent dread rise up from the now tainted wine, enveloping the situation in a soft embrace of laughter.

But let us not dwell solely on the misfortunes of star-crossed lovers and their oenophilic endeavors, for the confounding world of the comically botched uncorking extends far and wide into a plethora of equally amusing territories. Consider the response of our mighty cork, now under siege by a set of gnarled and seemingly inept hands, balking at the thought of being removed unceremoniously from its vinous prison, obfuscated as it is by layers of tissue, ribbon, plastic, wax, or glass. The unwitting guest at a dinner party who fumbles, tugs and hauls at an obstinate synthetic cork, much to the amusement and delight of their equally good-natured onlookers.

The ingenuity born from desperation and creative thinking evokes both admiration and bemusement in those who bear witness to the many manifestations of the uncorking catastrophe. The enlistment of pliers, shoes, boots, leaves, and even unwieldy configurations of wire coat hangers as makeshift weaponry against the indomitable cork heralds a new era of delightful madness and sublime lunacy. In these moments, the adage "necessity is the mother of invention" takes on a life of its own, a convivialness that brings us together in absurd triumphs and defeats.

Such disastrous feats of uncorking are not only confined to the domestic sphere among diners, wine enthusiasts, and party guests gloriously ripe for ridicule. Consider the professional realm, that bastion of unflappable composure and sartorial elegance, where all too often, the field is laid bare for the most unexpected of encounters with the insidious specter of corkage catastrophe. In a hushed boardroom, a desperate executive attempts – with slowly mounting terror – to dismantle a corkscrew ensnared within a crumbling remnant of cork, their pleas for aid met with the merciless titters of their unsympathetic comrades.

We are left, then, with the lasting memories – indelible, spellbinding vignettes that punctuate our collective oenophilic history with a flourish of creativity and disarray. Tales of torn cork innards, decapitated corkscrews, and embedded projectiles, forever intertwined with laughter, tears, and gallons of hastily repurposed wine – the bittersweet nectar of folly that underscores the human experience in all its intricate, chaotic glory.

Let us raise a proverbial glass to the catastrophes that have graced our oenophilic escapades and fueled our comical tales, for they are a testament to the indomitable spirit of human ingenuity and the inherent humor that lies at the heart of our wine-soaked experiences. Amid these stories of un-sprung corks and beleaguered corkscrews, may we find solace, camaraderie, and a resonance that unites us all in the shared understanding of respect, power, and mirth: the art of uncorking gone wildly awry.

Glass Half-Fool: Riotous Experiences with Choosing and Holding Wine Glasses

Once the fraught initial skirmish between human and cork has been waged, we enter a new arena of social and sartorial challenge: the half-filled, deceptively fluid realm of the wine glass. Perhaps no other utensil can summon such spectacular and flamboyant tales of wobbling feints, garbled decantings, and remarkable faux pas as this infinitely innocuous, yet astonishingly treacherous piece of stemware. Like the comically dauntless samurai of far-eastern lore, the glass – when raised, swilled, or tragically upended – dispenses its contents with a resolute air of either profound elegance or unmitigated disaster.

Consider the bewildingly vast and varied menagerie of glassware that exists today, each with its own quirks, curiosities, and potential for disaster. Burgundy, Bordeaux, or Sauvignon Blanc: although these names may evoke impressions of sun-drenched vineyards and bucolic sophistication, in reality, they bear testament to the dark side of wine tasting: the infinite litany of arcane and often mystifying glassware that accompanies each, standing proud as a flashing, brimming beacon of hilarity, humiliation, or both.

One can no more truly grasp the befuddling confusion of the uniquely-shaped, smoke-colored, and oftentimes towering wine glasses that proliferate throughout the world than one can entirely comprehend the nuances and complexities underlying the labyrinthine etiquette that surrounds them. This is a mysterious, treacherous web of rules, conventions, and unspoken signals, the like of which may well leave the unwary and uninitiated reeling beneath the weight of its imponderable absurdities.

Survey the fledgling oenophile as they approach, with quavering hand and barely-contained tremble, the bewildering array of delicate, fragile stemware that adorns the dining table before them, captured at once by the paradoxical spell of elegance and humour that bounds these most subtle of wine allies. Observe, now, as they struggle to ascertain the proper glass for each varietal, their efforts blighted by inexperience, overconfidence, and a stubborn conviction that no glass shall triumph over human will and wit.

The inadvertent descent into the realm of comedy begins when our intrepid protagonist selects the incorrect vessel – a towering monolith of crystal, perhaps, designed to capture and release the heady aroma of some deep, brooding red, now filled with a delicate, demure white that can only weep silently, its floral song stifled beneath the weight of its new-found home. With the equanimity of a master juggler, the terror-stricken imbiber grasps their chosen glass by the most inappropriate spot, fingers unwittingly wrapping themselves around the bulbous bowl, obscuring the delicate bloom of the wine within, and leaving a sticky trail of fingerprints as evidence of their passage. They proceed, undeterred, ignorant of the comical mishap that is unfolding before them.

A tidal wave of misfortune builds, as our unwitting hero tentatively raises the glass to their lips, navigating the perilous and unseen chasm between surface tension and equilibrium – a journey fraught with such uncertainty and tension that one may swear they felt the tremors of their grip emanating through the air. The ensuing deluge of fruit, alcohol, and airborne vinous laughter that reverberates around the room is a riotous counterpoint to the discomfited silence that follows, leaving the hapless victim to wallow in their newfound infamy.

Yet it is not merely inexperienced newcomers who are vulnerable to the caprices of this glassy gauntlet; as the layman's adage "never trust a known brand" warns, even the most accomplished wine connoisseurs may find themselves at the mercy of an insidious piece of stemware, with its barely perceptible imperfections or mischievous feints. Beautiful though they may be, the blowsy curves and sweeping lines of these fragile vessels can conspire to overcome logic and reason, luring their devoted admirers into a vortex of confusion that cannot, in this moment of ignominy, be traversed by any degree of experience or finesse.

As we depart the perfidious realm of the wine glass and its myriad soy traps, it falls to us to embrace its unwieldy imperfections, and to accept the unbridled chaos and humour that accompanies our attempts to master it. For in this dance of elegance and eccentricity, there lies a thread that binds us, again, to the joy of wine and the inimitable joys of a thousand clumsy glasses clutched, clinked, swilled, and sloshed. Like the fluid itself, these giddy delights may come and go in a torrent of uncertainty – but in acknowledging this precariousness, we may begin to forge our own unique and memorable path through the wine-soaked gatherings of time.

Awkward Aeration: Comically Fumbled Attempts at Decanting

A world apart from its austere cousin, the corkscrew, the decanter is an enigmatic and curious figure, its sinuous curves and beveled edges tracing an ancient lineage of wine preservation and pretention. Threading the fine line between highbrow ritual and hilarious blunder, the act of decanting wine represents both art form and fascinating foible—an opportunity for the archetypical sommelier to shine and the unwitting operator to fumble spectacularly.

We are but eager observers on the sidelines, witnessing the elegant ballet of decanting and the inextricable potential for comedy and misadventure that it offers. Where once the act of aeration was confined to dusty, cobwebbed cellars populated by the illustrious and ceremonial, it now finds itself in the hands of the everyman and woman—an integral yet maddeningly elusive component in the wild and riotous carnival of wine appreciation.

One imagines the first furtive overtures of this delicate dance: the tentative pouring of a Chateau Neuf-du-Pape, sequestered away in the darkest recesses of one's ancestral home, into a crystal decanter so fine and fragile that it seems to quiver at the very thought of being used for this most holy of purposes. The heartfelt swish and swoop of the wine through this translucent, hourglass amphitheater is enough to send shivers down the spine of even the most calloused and withered of oenophiles.

Yet it is here, in this sacred moment, that comedy finds its opportunity to strike. For the uninitiated, decanting is not a science but a fool's errand, a series of harrowing and oftentimes panicked attempts to coax forth the sanguine contents of a lavishly adorned bottle without invoking the ire of its thousand-year-old spirit. The vagaries of pouring position, rotation, and glass type merge with the hypochondriac fear of shattering this most hallowed of vessels or worse still, drowning it in the swirling deluge of unprepared wine.

From the precipice of calamity emerge scenes of the most absurd and entrancing hilarity. How shall we console the inexperienced amateur, trembling at the thought of aeration, as they clasp their wine bottle tightly to their chest, seeking comfort and solace from this time-honored ritual? Equally, what words of comfort assist the gleeful optimist whose swift and dexterous pouring technique bears disastrous result, forming a wholly unanticipated cascade of ruby red down the neck of the decanter and onto the once pristine tablecloth below?

Such beautiful, tragic folly is not confined only to the intimacy of domestic gatherings. Indeed, some of the most triumphant and confounding examples of decanting debacles can be found within the impenetrable annals of illustrious society, where wine and wealth commingle in a shimmering tableau of excess and ridicule. Picture the august setting of a vast and venerable chateau, acting as a silent witness to the escalating blushes and expressions of smug amusement that color the cheeks of its dinner guests, as wine is inexpertly aerated with all the finesse of a charging rhinoceros.

Even the most sacred of ceremonies are not exempt from the devious charms of the decanter. The hushed stillness of a black-tie charity event provides an ideal backdrop for the consternation and barely concealed snickers that greet the sight of a helpless guest, struggling to understand the complex spatial requirements of pouring out of a cumbersome amphora and into a bewildering tangle of crystal stemware.

Such incidents of heartfelt absurdity serve to remind us that within the act of decanting lies an inexhaustible source of mirth and marvel, an ever-expanding assemblage of pratfalls, fumbles, and misadventures that, like drops of water in an ever-fulling decanter, mirror the complexities and absurdities of our own lives.

So let us raise our half-filled goblets to these moments of unquenchable laughter and despair, these instances when polished perfection is buried beneath a torrent of comical disarray. As we gingerly inch our way toward a mastery of this arcane and comical rite, may we find within ourselves the courage to laugh and learn from our decanting delirium – lest we too find ourselves soaked by the unpredictable and fascinating whims of wine aerated in less-than-graceful splendor.

Snorting and Sniffing: Amusing Anecdotes on Smelling Wine Before Sipping

As our hapless initiates into the sprawling world of wine grapple valiantly with corkscrews and quavering wine glasses, they encounter a ritual that bridges the realms of intoxicating seriousness and high comic farce: the olfactory appreciation of wine, or, as it is more colloquially known, the art of sniffing. This, dear reader, is an act that calls forth wonders, miracles, and metaphors of all manner of construction and ethereal fragility; but, most importantly, it is a wellspring of endless amusement, characterised by ellipses of earthly and divine fragrance.

To navigate the breathless, uncharted terrain of winy redolence with any manner of grace, one must first relinquish the mortal pretence of serious-mindedness and embrace the quixotic, vaguely absurd notion of appraising, describing, and – yes – inhaling wines with the rapacious ardour of an amateur sleuth. Dauntless, unapologetic, and ridden with an unspoken malaise of self-doubt, our earnest wine sniffer plunges headlong into the mystifying fray, nostrils quivering with anticipation and fear.

Watch now, as a young, neophyte enologist approaches the glass with the comical, exaggerated hauteur of a fledgling dancer, striving vainly to reconcile the equally elusive principles of weightlessness and gravitas as they gingerly lower their face to the gaping maw of the glass, swathed in all its treacherous allure. Eyes squeezed tight, head cocked at an ungainly angle, nostrils flaring – here, my friends, we stand, united in our invisible tapestry of laughter, as our unfortunate novice negotiates their way through the Scylla and Charybdis of the wine world, the roaring seas of chardonnay and sun-dappled beaches of pinot noir.

Our story cannot end here, though! For while unspoken amusement and subterranean joy may bind us in our collective mirth as we stroll the fragrant pathways of vinous enquiry, surely there is room, too, for a more edifying and uplifting view of these uncharted horticultural byways. Amidst the strangled pauses, shuffling footwork, and tentative sniffs, there swirls a riot of language: a cacophonous parade of adjectival excess and lyrical indulgence.

Wine, we are told, may smell of autumn leaves, of afternoon sunshine, of the blown kisses of a thousand sleeping roses. It can evoke images of distant woodland glades, of leather-bound libraries, and tempest-tossed seas – or the haze-steeped, jasmine-touched pathways of a Moorish courtyard.

As aspirational sommeliers and amateur wine lovers alike, we are invited, nay, compelled, to traverse this linguistic minefield with the same ungainly grace and aplomb as our hapless subject might attempt to conquer the fragrant abyss of the wine glass. We must not merely drink the wine but swallow whole the universe it purports to contain, rejoicing in the rich tapestry of sensory description that surrounds us on all sides.

Beyond the veil of linguistic and sensory frivolity, there exists still further room for humour and self-deprecation. For it seems as though the ritual of inhaling wine aroma is entirely dependent on the elusive and intangible virtue of timing – or more precisely, the impossibility of predicting the exact moment at which a sip (or sniff) of wine may transform from a most blissful, cerebral experience to a jarring, corporeal realisation of human frailty.

Take, for example, the entirely relatable and deeply amusing moment when our good-hearted wine enthusiast – buoyed by the confidence that only a burgeoning understanding of the complexities of oenophily can inspire – approaches the glass with a newly learned knowledge that plunging one's nose into the bouquet is a laudatory act of bravado, signalling one's commitment to the fine task. Imagine their eyes widening with terror and embarrassment as the heady scent of ripe fruits, polished oak, and sighing petals is momentarily usurped by the searing heat of alcohol, an olfactory onslaught that sends tears streaming and knees buckling in a most uncontrolled and undignified manner. So endeth the lesson in the true hazards of wine sniffing.

As we depart from the fragrant embrace of temptuous, flame-touched wines, let us remember – with a heart full of mirth and a mind braced against the encroaching tide of self-doubt – that the act of sniffing may well represent the most capricious of all wine rituals, a nexus of happenstance and laughter that brings warmth and humanity to a realm otherwise dominated by the august, the esoteric, and the absurdly priced. It might come as a perfect reminder that grace and curiosity are but transient gifts, and that in stepping from the teetering precipice of the unknown to the intoxicating opulence of the unlabeled, we might yet find ourselves laughing arm in arm towards enlightenment. For somewhere between the first tentative sniff and the final astonished gasp lies a kingdom of simple, unfettered joy that transcends the boundaries of social convention, taste, and vintage – the pure, unburdened pleasure of discovering, naming, and sharing the ineffable whispers of a thousand unseen glassy wonders.

Swirling Slip-ups: Navigating Wine Swirling Without Splashing or Staining

As we embark upon a voyage steeped in the treacherous waters of wine swirling, we find ourselves precariously balanced on a cliff's edge, toes curling in anticipation of the gusty winds of fortune that might carry us to safety—or perhaps plunge us headlong into an inky abyss of disgrace and staining. We are like fledgling birds poised on the very cusp of flight, the wine glass our veritable trapeze, where dazzling virtuosity and catastrophic plunges from grace coexist in a delicate dance of reckless abandon and majestic resplendence.

Picture, if you will, the unsuspecting novice, bravely attempting to replicate the deftly executed spiraling of a crystal goblet that they had observed in a neighbouring soiree. Hands trembling with a mixture of excitement and trepidation, they furiously attempt to oscillate their glass, only to fling the silky, inviting contents of a prized Merlot from its elegant confines in a glorious, haphazard effusion of grandiosity. The dripping vestiges bear witness to a moment of chimerical enthusiasm, a grin that turned too quickly into a grimace, an instant when the tantalizing brush of unadulterated glamour crumbled into ashen parody.

Here, my friends, we encounter the very essence of swirling slip-ups – a litany of fumbled attempts, ruined table linens, and bewildered, ink-stained smiles as we navigate the treacherous path from eager instructional video enthusiast to seasoned oenophile. Although this tale may be tinged with an edge of wistfulness and soggy desperation, it also presents a wondrous tableau of human ingenuity, creativity, and unadulterated glee.

Consider, for instance, the aspiring wine aficionado who, realizing that their attempts at swirling are only yielding a series of confused and stuttering gyrations, resorts to implementing a number of innovative techniques, including cradling the base of their glass in the seashell-like contours of their palm or attempting to harness the kinetic energy of a well-timed hip thrust. Their determination and resourcefulness in mastering this elusive art coaxes a bubble of laughter to rise within our throats, a silent litany of admiration and solidarity offered across the widening expanse of spilled wine and tear-streaked tablecloths.

Perhaps the most poignant of all swirling misadventures, however, is the unintentional slapstick comedy that arises in moments of sheer overexuberance. Picture the scene: the bold and brazen wine enthusiast, filled with self-assurance as the heady scent of grape-infused magic wafts upward from their glass, suddenly captured by a giddy impulse to swirl with such frenetic energy that not only their wine but their very universe is set to spinning. As the centrifugal force is unleashed, it becomes clear that such bacchanalian exuberance might indeed know no bounds, and, as the shimmering pool of costly nectar expands across the pale expanse of a once-immaculate tablecloth, we cannot help but join hands in a shared hymn of laughter and commiseration.

It is given to us, the fortunate and the bold, to stride bravely into the swirling landscape and emerge unscathed or, at the very least, on speaking terms with our dry cleaners. The path forward may be shrouded in the umbral gloom of uncertainty and bespattered with the blood-red stains of misguided folly, but it is a journey that offers not only insight into the swirling mysteries of wine appreciation but also an exquisite opportunity for the sharing of laughter, the pooling of camaraderie, and the tender outpouring of support that only a shared, crimson catastrophe can evoke.

As we move ever closer towards true refinement, each swirling stumble is, in its own way, an expression of life in all its raw, unadulterated splendor. Our footprints may be stained, our laughter strained, our spirits dampened by the weight of unmet expectation—but within these velvet mountains of spilled wine lies a harvest of potential, a path leading towards redemption and the crackling warmth of a newfound sense of camaraderie. Let us raise our soiled glasses in a toast to the swirling solace borne of collective misadventure and the shared kinship lurking within the darkest crevices of each wayward, crimson droplet.

Wine Party Whimsy: Entertaining Stories of Wine-Soaked Social Gatherings

In vino veritas, so the saying goes, and as the evening melts into night and wine after wine is generously and enthusiastically uncorked – fueling a symphony of wild laughter, fumbling embraces, and discordant serenades – the euphoria of unbound camaraderie rarely fails to materialize. But what precisely begets this arrival of such bacchanalian brotherhood? What makes these wine-soaked social gatherings such beacons of levity, lightness, and lovely whimsy?

The answer, dear reader, is deceptively simple: it is amidst these swirling, sloshing moments that we set aside the stiff formalities and unspoken social codes which govern our daily lives and instead succumb wholeheartedly to the rapturous joys of the unexpected, the absurd, and the unquestionably amusing.

In our meandering exploration through a world of wine, it is in these raucous, sparkling soirées that we truly witness the unbridled alchemy of the grape, as it converts not merely ordinary juice into a heady, intoxicating elixir, but ordinary people – each burdened by their own litany of fears, doubts, and insecurities – into convivial comrades, united in laughter, curiosity, and an overwhelming desire to connect and share in the bounty of the vine.

To fully appreciate the multifaceted gifts of these moments, allow us to journey through the intoxicating maze of wine party whimsy, as we explore the myriad fables, follies, and marvels that unfold within these enchanted realms.

A subtle murmur of anticipation fills the air as the first timid staccato notes of laughter escape the lips of the unsuspecting host – for there, nestled amongst the ravishing array of tantalizing tipple, lies the unassuming genesis of countless mirthful exchanges. Too often overlooked, it is the wine itself that warrants our deepest appreciation, as we marvel at the droplets of liquid sunshine, sombre ruby or blush-tinged rose that adorns the table – each hue the herald of an emerging tale of absurdity and delight.

In the cozy recesses of the dimly lit room, the soft glow of candlelight bathes our besotted companions in warm radiance, as the evening's libations begin their slow unraveling of inhibitions and guile. A newcomer to the enigmatic world of oenophilia tentatively bridges the gap between tentative reserve and eager enthusiasm, channeling their inner sommelier to pronounce a Shiraz as harboring "notes of blackberry compote, whispers of cinnamon, and an unmistakable overtone of playground asphalt after a summer rain."

The delighted gasps and chortles that ripple across the room attest to the magical power of wine to inspire not merely artistic verbosity but also the warm embrace of our shared humanity, as each individual – regardless of their carnal knowledge of Cabernet or familiarity with the vagaries of the Viognier – is welcomed into the fold with open arms and a foaming, relinquishing of judgment.

As the evening unfolds in a whirlwind of impromptu speeches, wine-fueled expressions of adoration, and clumsy yet endearing attempts at grape-centered trivia, it is through the eyes of the wine that we truly recognize the pure elemental magic it embodies. Lightning in a bottle, as it were – a conduit to a world of spontaneity, laughter, and an unencumbered outpouring of self-expression.

And oh, the tales we weave, in the tangled, lilting throes of wine-induced fancy! The moment when the soft-spoken teetotaler, sensing their destiny ripple through the room like a tremor, heeds the call of a majestic Sauternes and embraces their turn in the spotlight, showering their fellow revelers with warbling renditions of their favorite operatic arias, their newfound stage presence both astounding and hilarious to their audience.

A comically ardent debate erupts between fervent partisans of Merlot and Malbec, each regaling the enchanted crowd with tales of vinous victory and ruined epicurean masterpieces, their voices rising and arms flailing in a compelling display of passion that sparks both uproarious laughter and sudden, warm declarations of unity amongst the otherwise-entrenched factions.

In these moments of inebriated insight, it becomes clear that the majesty of wine lies not merely in its tantalizing aromas, the rich tapestry of flavors it gifts our palates, or even the glittering display of amethyst, amber, and obsidian that bedecks our tables, but rather the singular, priceless privilege of basking in the glow of raw, unfiltered human connection – the sparkling tapestry of laughter, curiosity, and vulnerability that only the free-flowing caress of the vine can awaken within us all.

So raise your glass, dear reader, to toast the unforgettable, absurd, and heartwarming ways in which wine enables us to weave our varied threads into a single, shimmering tapestry of joy, wonder, and endearing folly.